W9-CKH-787

CIVIL LIBERTIES

OPPOSING VIEWPOINTS®

David L. Bender & Bruno Leone, *Series Editors*

Julie S. Bach, *Book Editor*
Neal Bernards, Lynn Hall, Mary Teresa O'Neill, *Assistant Editors*

OPPOSING VIEWPOINTS SERIES ®

Greenhaven Press   577 Shoreview Park Road   St. Paul, Minnesota 55126

Library of Congress Cataloging-in-Publication Data

Civil liberties, opposing viewpoints / Julie S. Bach, book editor,
   Neal Bernards, Lynn Hall, Terry O'Neill, assistant editors.
      p.   cm. — (Opposing viewpoint series)
   Bibliography: p.
   Includes index.
   ISBN 0-89908-409-5   (pbk.) : $6.95. ISBN 0-89908-434-6
(lib. bdg.) : $13.95
     1. Civil rights. I. Bach, Julie S., 1963-   . II.
Bernards, Neal, 1963-   . III. Hall, Lynn,
1949-   . IV.
O'Neill, Terry, 1944-   . V. Series.
JCS71.C592 1988
323.4—dc19   88-1136
                                   CIP

"Congress shall make no law...
abridging the freedom of speech,
or of the press."

First Amendment to the US Constitution

The basic foundation of our democracy is the first amendment
guarantee of freedom of expression. The *Opposing Viewpoints Series*
is dedicated to the concept of this basic freedom and the idea that
it is more important to practice it than to enshrine it.

Contents

Chapter 3: How Free Should Speech Be?

Chapter 4: What Violates the Right to Privacy?

Why Consider Opposing Viewpoints?

"It is better to debate a question without settling it than to settle a question without debating it."

Joseph Joubert (1754-1824)

The Importance of Examining Opposing Viewpoints

The purpose of the Opposing Viewpoints Series, and this book in particular, is to present balanced, and often difficult to find, opposing points of view on complex and sensitive issues.

Probably the best way to become informed is to analyze the positions of those who are regarded as experts and well studied on issues. It is important to consider every variety of opinion in an attempt to determine the truth. Opinions from the mainstream of society should be examined. But also important are opinions that are considered radical, reactionary, or minority as well as those stigmatized by some other uncomplimentary label. An important lesson of history is the eventual acceptance of many unpopular and even despised opinions. The ideas of Socrates, Jesus, and Galileo are good examples of this.

Readers will approach this book with their own opinions on the issues debated within it. However, to have a good grasp of one's own viewpoint, it is necessary to understand the arguments of those with whom one disagrees. It can be said that those who do not completely understand their adversary's point of view do not fully understand their own.

A persuasive case for considering opposing viewpoints has been presented by John Stuart Mill in his work *On Liberty*. When examining controversial issues it may be helpful to reflect on this suggestion:

> The only way in which a human being can make some approach to knowing the whole of a subject, is by hearing what can be said about it by persons of every variety of opinion, and studying all modes in which it can be looked at by every character of mind. No wise man ever acquired his wisdom in any mode but this.

Analyzing Sources of Information

The Opposing Viewpoints Series includes diverse materials taken from magazines, journals, books, and newspapers, as well as statements and position papers from a wide range of individuals, organizations and governments. This broad spectrum of sources helps to develop patterns of thinking which are open to the consideration of a variety of opinions.

Pitfalls To Avoid

A pitfall to avoid in considering opposing points of view is that of regarding one's own opinion as being common sense and the most rational stance and the point of view of others as being only opinion and naturally wrong. It may be that another's opinion is correct and one's own is in error.

Another pitfall to avoid is that of closing one's mind to the opinions of those with whom one disagrees. The best way to approach a dialogue is to make one's primary purpose that of understanding the mind and arguments of the other person and not that of enlightening him or her with one's own solutions. More can be learned by listening than speaking.

It is my hope that after reading this book the reader will have a deeper understanding of the issues debated and will appreciate the complexity of even seemingly simple issues on which good and honest people disagree. This awareness is particularly important in a democratic society such as ours where people enter into public debate to determine the common good. Those with whom one disagrees should not necessarily be regarded as enemies, but perhaps simply as people who suggest different paths to a common goal.

Developing Basic Reading and Thinking Skills

In this book, carefully edited opposing viewpoints are purposely placed back to back to create a running debate; each viewpoint is preceded by a short quotation that best expresses the author's main argument. This format instantly plunges the reader into the midst of a controversial issue and greatly aids that reader in mastering the basic skill of recognizing an author's point of view.

A number of basic skills for critical thinking are practiced in the activities that appear throughout the books in the series. Some of the skills are:

Evaluating Sources of Information   The ability to choose from among alternative sources the most reliable and accurate source in relation to a given subject.

Separating Fact from Opinion   The ability to make the basic distinction between factual statements (those that can be demonstrated or verified empirically) and statements of opinion (those that are beliefs or attitudes that cannot be proved).

Identifying Stereotypes   The ability to identify oversimplified, exaggerated descriptions (favorable or unfavorable) about people and insulting statements about racial, religious or national groups, based upon misinformation or lack of information.

Recognizing Ethnocentrism   The ability to recognize attitudes or opinions that express the view that one's own race, culture, or group is inherently superior, or those attitudes that judge another culture or group in terms of one's own.

It is important to consider opposing viewpoints and equally important to be able to critically analyze those viewpoints. The activities in this book are designed to help the reader master these thinking skills. Statements are taken from the book's viewpoints and the reader is asked to analyze them. This technique aids the reader in developing skills that not only can be applied to the viewpoints in this book, but also to situations where opinionated spokespersons comment on controversial issues. Although the activities are helpful to the solitary reader, they are most useful when the reader can benefit from the interaction of group discussion.

Using this book and others in the series should help readers develop basic reading and thinking skills. These skills should improve the reader's ability to understand what they read. Readers should be better able to separate fact from opinion, substance from rhetoric and become better consumers of information in our media-centered culture.

This volume of the Opposing Viewpoints Series does not advocate a particular point of view. Quite the contrary! The very nature of the book leaves it to the reader to formulate the opinions he or she finds most suitable. My purpose as publisher is to see that this is made possible by offering a wide range of viewpoints which are fairly presented.

David L. Bender
Publisher

11

Introduction

On any given day, in any newspaper in the United States, readers are likely to come across the word *rights* in stories about issues from economics to sex. The Ku Klux Klan claims the right to speak at a political rally; minorities demand the right to equal employment; workers claim the right not to be tested for drug use. Perhaps more than any people in the world, Americans are obsessed with their rights. They carefully define them and fight for them, but in a country of over two hundred million people, the definitions vary greatly. Those differing definitions of civil liberties may even lead to conflict.

An airline incident in 1988 illustrates how passionately Americans will fight for the least of their rights. When a pilot banned smoking on a TWA flight from Boston to Los Angeles, some of the passengers smoked anyway. These passengers felt the rule was an infringement on their right to smoke. The non-smoking passengers thought the lit cigarettes were an infringement on their right to breathe clean air. A fight broke out when the flight attendants attempted to enforce the pilot's ban. The disturbance prompted the pilot to radio for police to be waiting in Los Angeles in case they were needed to arrest the troublemakers.

Although the Bill of Rights mentions nothing about clean air or smoking, its legacy of concern for liberty infuses even these seemingly minor debates. Some of the founders of the democracy, such as Alexander Hamilton, feared that placing an emphasis on protecting individual rights would result in chaotic disregard for order, as the TWA episode seems to reflect. He believed that the people could not be entirely trusted to put the common good above their own concerns.

Thomas Jefferson, on the other hand, believed nothing was more important than individual rights. He was confident that the

13

American people would act responsibly with the freedom they were given and was horrified at the thought of government curtailing the rights of an individual. His is the philosophy reflected by the common American refrain, "I demand my rights."

That the struggle over civil liberties has never lessened is testimony to the strong sense of rights Americans have. The conflicts presented in *Civil Liberties: Opposing Viewpoints* reflect that passion for liberty. The book opens with a chapter of historical debates by some of America's most influential political and literary figures. Other topics covered are: Should the Church and the State Remain Separate? How Free Should Speech Be? What Violates the Right to Privacy? and Is the Government Responsible for Securing Minority Rights? As in all Opposing Viewpoints books, readers are left to draw their own conclusions on what constitutes liberty and how those liberties should be protected.

Historical Debates on Civil Liberties

Chapter Preface

In 1791, John Quincy Adams wrote: "Happy, thrice happy the people of America! ... whose equal representation in their legislative councils was founded upon an equality really existing among them, and not upon the metaphysical speculations of fanciful politicians." Adams believed that all people were endowed with inalienable rights and that the function of government was to protect these fundamental rights, not give them. Adams and his contemporaries based the Declaration of Independence, the Constitution, and the Bill of Rights on this idea of inherent equality. They fought and died believing that in America, for the first time in the world's history, people would be guaranteed true freedom.

The colonists, however, did not always agree on how freedom was to be achieved: They disagreed with one another as bitterly as politicians do today. It was their debates, however, that contributed to the ideals that founded American democracy. Their essays, pamphlets, and letters form a rich resource on liberty and equality. The viewpoints in this chapter are culled from this reservoir of political thought. They provide examples of the debate that has helped to shape the civil liberties enjoyed by Americans today.

"The right of colonists to exercise a legislative power, is no natural right."

Liberty Is Guaranteed Under the King's Rule

Samuel Seabury

Many people in the American colonies did not want independence from England. In the following viewpoint, one of these loyalists, a New York clergyman named Samuel Seabury, replies to a speech made by Alexander Hamilton at the Continental Congress. Though his reply, published in 1774, is addressed specifically to Hamilton, it expresses the view of many colonists in that period that liberty would be better secured by remaining under British rule.

As you read, consider the following questions:

1. Why does Seabury prefer being governed by England?
2. According to the author, why is it an impropriety to speak of an "independent colony"?
3. How does Seabury react to the argument that the colonies have a right to independence only if England makes laws without their consent?

Samuel Seabury, "A View of the Controversy, &c. in A Letter to the Author of *A Full Vindication, &c.*" in *Letters of a Westchester Farmer*. London: Richardson and Urquhart, 1775.

You have taken some pains to prove what would readily have been granted you—that *liberty* is a very *good* thing, and *slavery* is a very *bad* thing. But when I must think that liberty under a *King, Lords,* and *Commons* is as good as liberty under a republican Congress: And that slavery under a republican Congress is as bad, at least, as slavery under a *King, Lords* and *Commons:* And upon the whole, that *liberty* under the supreme authority and protection of Great-Britain, is infinitely preferable to *slavery* under an American Congress. I will also agree with you, "that Americans are intitled to freedom." I will go further: I will own and acknowledge that not only *Americans,* but *Africans, Europeans, Asiaticks,* all men, of all countries and degrees, of all sizes and complexions, have a right to as much freedom as is consistent with the security of civil society: And I hope you will not think me an "enemy to the *natural* rights of mankind" because I cannot wish them more. We must however remember, that more liberty may, without inconvenience, be allowed to individuals in a small government, than can be admitted of in a large empire.

But when you assert that "since Americans have not by any act of theirs impowered the British parliament to make laws for them, it follows they can have no just authority to do it," you advance a position subversive of that dependence which all colonies must, from their very nature, have on the mother country.—By the British parliament, I suppose you mean the supreme legislative authority, the King, Lords and Commons, because no other authority in England has a right to make laws to bind the kingdom, and consequently no authority to make laws to bind the colonies. In this sense I shall understand, and use the phrase *British parliament.*

Now the dependence of the colonies on the mother-country has ever been acknowledged. It is an impropriety of speech to talk of an independent colony. The words *independency* and *colony,* convey contradictory ideas: much like *killing* and *sparing.* As soon as a colony becomes independent on its parent state, it ceases to be any longer a colony; just as when you *kill* a sheep, you cease to *spare* him. The British colonies make a part of the British Empire. As parts of the body they must be subject to the general laws of the body. To talk of a colony independent of the mother-country, is no better sense than to talk of a limb independent of the body to which it belongs.

A Supreme Authority

In every government there must be a supreme, absolute authority lodged somewhere. In arbitrary governments this power is in the monarch; in aristocratical governments, in the nobles; in democratical, in the people; or the deputies of their electing. Our own government being a mixture of all these kinds, the supreme authority is vested in the King, Nobles and People, i.e. the King, House of Lords, and House of Commons elected by the people. This supreme authority extends as far as the British dominions extend. To suppose a part of the British dominions which is not subject to the power of the British legislature, is no better sense than to suppose a country, at one and the same time, to be, and not to be a part of the British dominions, if therefore the colony of New-York be a part of the British dominions, the colony of New-York is subject, and dependent on the supreme legislative authority of Great-Britain.

Legislation is not an inherent right in the colonies. Many colonies have been established, and subsisted long without it. The Roman colonies had no legislative authority. It was not till the later period of their republic that the privileges of Roman citizens, among which that of voting in the assemblies of the people at Rome was a principal one, were extended to the inhabitants of Italy. All the laws of the empire were enacted at Rome. Neither their colonies, nor conquered countries had any thing to do with legislation.

Authority of God

It is under the deputation and authority of God alone that *kings reign and princes decree justice.* Kings and princes (which are only other words for supreme magistrates) were doubtless created and appointed, not so much for their own sakes, as for the sake of the people committed to their charge: yet are they not, therefore, the creatures of the people. So far from deriving their authority from any supposed consent or suffrage of men, they receive their commission from Heaven.

Jonathan Boucher, *A View of the Causes and Consequences of the American Revolution,* 1797.

The position that we are bound by no laws to which we have not consented, either by ourselves, or our representatives, is a novel position, unsupported by any authoritative record of the British constitution, ancient or modern. It is republican in its very nature, and tends to the utter subversion of the English monarchy.

This position has arisen from an artful change of terms. To say that an Englishman is not bound by any laws, but those to which the representatives of the nation have given their consent, is to say what is true: But to say that an Englishman is bound by no laws but those to which *he* hath consented in person, or by *his* representative, is saying what never was true, and never can be true. A great part of the people in England have no vote in the choice of representatives, and therefore are governed by laws to which they never consented either by *themselves* or by *their* representatives.

The right of colonists to exercise a legislative power, is no natural right. They derive it not from nature, but from the indulgence or grant of the parent state, whose subjects they were when the colony was settled, and by whose permission and assistance they made the settlement.

Upon supposition that every English colony enjoyed a legislative power independent of the parliament; and that the parliament has no just authority to make laws to bind them, this absurdity will follow—that there is no power in the British empire, which has authority to make laws for the whole empire; i.e. we have an empire, without government; or which amounts to the same thing, we have a government which has no supreme power. All our colonies are independent of each other: Suppose them independent of the British parliament,—what power do you leave to govern the whole? None at all. You split and divide the empire into a number of petty insignificant states. This is the direct, the necessary tendency of refusing submission to acts of parliament. Every man who can see one inch beyond his nose, must see this consequence. And every man who endeavours to accelerate the independency of the colonies on the British parliament, endeavours to accelerate the ruin of the British empire.

Authority and Obedience

To talk of being liege subjects to King George, while we disavow the authority of parliament is another piece of whiggish nonsense. I love my King as well as any whig in America or England either, and am as ready to yield him all lawful submission: But while I submit to the King, I submit to the authority of the laws of the state, whose guardian the King is. The difference between a good and a bad subject, is only this, that the one obeys, the other transgresses the law. The difference between a loyal subject and a rebel, is, that the one yields obedience to, and faithfully supports the supreme authority of the state, and the other endeavours to overthrow it. If we obey the laws of the King, we obey the laws of the parliament. If we disown the authority of the parliament, we disown the authority of King. There is no medium without ascribing powers to the King which the constitution knows nothing of:— without making him superior to the laws, and setting him above all restraint. These are some of the ridiculous absurdities of American whiggism.

*"Whenever any form of government becomes
destructive of these ends [life, liberty, and the
pursuit of happiness], it is the right of the
people to alter or abolish it."*

Liberty Can Only Be Achieved by Independent Rule

Thomas Jefferson

Thomas Jefferson, third president of the United States, was the
principal author of the Declaration of Independence. His first draft
of that document is reprinted in the following viewpoint. Jefferson's version differs slightly from the one finally adopted by the
Continental Congress in 1776, but no less eloquently expresses
his belief that the American people would achieve true liberty only
if they govern themselves.

As you read, consider the following questions:

1. Why does Jefferson believe it necessary to declare the
   reasons for separation from England?
2. What truths does Jefferson call self-evident? Why are these
   truths important to the Declaration of Independence?
3. According to the author, what did the colonists hope to
   achieve by independent rule?

Thomas Jefferson, "The Declaration of Independence," *The Works of Thomas Jefferson, I.*
New York: G.P. Putnam's Sons, 1904.

When in the course of human events it becomes necessary for one people to dissolve the political bands which have connected them with another, and to assume among the powers of the earth the separate & equal station to which the laws of nature and of nature's God entitle them, a decent respect to the opinions of mankind requires that they should declare the causes which impel them to the separation.

We hold these truths to be self-evident: that all men are created equal; that they are endowed by their creator with inherent and inalienable rights; that among these are life, liberty, & the pursuit of happiness: that to secure these rights, governments are instituted among men, deriving their just powers from the consent of the governed; that whenever any form of government becomes destructive of these ends, it is the right of the people to alter or abolish it, & to institute new government, laying it's foundation on such principles, & organizing it's powers in such form, as to them shall seem most likely to effect their safety & happiness. Prudence indeed will dictate that governments long established should not be changed for light & transient causes; and accordingly all experience hath shown that mankind is more disposed to suffer while evils are sufferable, than to right themselves by abolishing the forms to which they are accustomed. But when a long train of abuses & usurpations begun at a distinguished period and pursuing invariably the same object, evinces a design to reduce them under absolute despotism, it is their right, it is their duty to throw off such government, & to provide new guards for their future security. Such has been the patient sufferance of these colonies; & such is now the necessity which constrains them to expunge their former systems of government. The history of the present king of Great Britain is a history of unremitting injuries & usurpations, among which appears no solitary fact to contradict the uniform tenor of the rest but all have in direct object the establishment of an absolute tyranny over these states. To prove this let facts be submitted to a candid world for the truth of which we pledge a faith yet unsullied by falsehood.

A List of Injuries

He has refused his assent to laws the most wholesome & necessary for the public good.

He has forbidden his governors to pass laws of immediate & pressing importance, unless suspended in their operation till his assent should be obtained; & when so suspended, he has utterly neglected to attend to them.

He has refused to pass other laws for the accommodation of large districts of people, unless those people would relinquish the right of representation in the legislature, a right inestimable to them, & formidable to tyrants only.

He has called together legislative bodies at places unusual, un-comfortable, and distant from the despository of their public records, for the sole purpose of fatiguing them into compliance with his measures.

He has dissolved representative houses repeatedly & continually for opposing with manly firmness his invasions on the rights of the people.

He has refused for a long time after such dissolutions to cause others to be elected, whereby the legislative powers, incapable of annihilation, have returned to the people at large for their ex-ercise, the state remaining in the meantime exposed to all the dangers of invasion from without & convulsions within.

He has endeavored to prevent the population of these states; for that purpose obstructing the laws for naturalization of foreigners, refusing to pass others to encourage their migrations hither, & raising the conditions of new appropriations of lands.

He has suffered the administration of justice totally to cease in some of these states refusing his assent to laws for establishing judiciary powers.

Nothing But Independence

Nothing but independence, *i.e.* a Continental form of government, can keep the peace of the Continent and preserve it inviolate from civil wars. I dread the event of a reconciliation with Britain now, as it is more than probable that it will be followed by a revolt some-where or other, the consequences of which may be far more fatal than all the malice of Britain.

Thomas Paine, *Common Sense*, 1776.

He has made our judges dependent on his will alone, for the tenure of their offices, & the amount & paiment of their salaries.

He has erected a multitude of new offices by a self assumed power and sent hither swarms of new officers to harass our people and eat out their substance.

He has kept among us in times of peace standing armies and ships of war without the consent of our legislatures.

He has affected to render the military independent of, & superior to the civil power.

Foreign to Our Laws

He has combined with others to subject us to a jurisdiction foreign to our constitutions & unacknowledged by our laws, giv-ing his assent to their acts of pretended legislation for quartering large bodies of armed troops among us; for protecting them by a mock-trial from punishment for any murders which they should commit on the inhabitants of these states; for cutting off our trade with all parts of the world; for imposing taxes on us without our consent; for depriving us of the benefits of trial by jury; for transporting us beyond seas to be tried for pretended offences; for abolishing the free system of English laws in a neighboring province, establishing therein an arbitrary government, and enlarging it's boundaries, so as to render it at once an example and fit instrument for introducing the same absolute rule into these states; for taking away our charters, abolishing our most valuable laws, and altering fundamentally the forms of our governments; for suspending our own legislatures, & declaring themselves invested with power to legislate for us in all cases whatsoever.

Out of His Allegiance

He has abdicated government here withdrawing his governors, and declaring us out of his allegiance & protection.

He has plundered our seas, ravaged our coasts, burnt our towns, & destroyed the lives of our people.

He is at this time transporting large armies of foreign mercenaries to compleat the works of death, desolation & tyranny already begun with circumstances of cruelty and perfidy unworthy the head of a civilized nation.

He has constrained our fellow citizens taken captive on the high seas to bear arms against their country, to become the executioners of their friends & brethren, or to fall themselves by their hands.

He has endeavored to bring on the inhabitants of our frontiers the merciless Indian savages, whose known rule of warfare is an undistinguished destruction of all ages, sexes, & conditions of existence.

He has incited treasonable insurrections of our fellow-citizens, with the allurements of forfeiture & confiscation of our property.

He has waged cruel war against human nature itself, violating it's most sacred rights of life and liberty in the persons of a distant people who never offended him, captivating & carrying them into slavery in another hemisphere, or to incur miserable death in their transportation thither. This piratical warfare, the opprobium of INFIDEL powers, is the warfare of the CHRISTIAN king of Great Britain. Determined to keep open a market where MEN should be bought & sold, he has prostituted his negative for suppressing every legislative attempt to prohibit or to restrain this execrable commerce. And that this assemblage of horrors might want no fact of distinguished die, he is now exciting those very people to rise in arms among us, and to purchase that liberty of which he has deprived them, by murdering the people on whom he also obtruded them: thus paying off former crimes committed against the LIBERTIES of one people, with crimes which he urges them to commit against the LIVES of another.

In every stage of these oppressions we have petitioned for redress in the most humble terms: our repeated petitions have been answered only by repeated injuries.

A prince whose character is thus marked by every act which may define a tyrant is unfit to be the ruler of a people who mean to be free. Future ages will scarcely believe that the hardiness of one man adventured, within the short compass of twelve years only, to lay a foundation so broad & so undisguised for tyranny over a people fostered & fixed in principles of freedom.

No Alternative

The colonies were taxed internally and externally; their essential interests sacrificed to individuals in Great-Britain; their legislatures suspended; charters annulled; trials by juries taken away; their persons subjected to transportation across the Atlantic, and to trial before foreign judicatories; their supplications for redress thought beneath answer; themselves published as cowards in the councils of their mother country and courts of Europe; armed troops sent among them to enforce submission to these violences; and actual hostilities commenced against them. No alternative was presented but resistance.

Thomas Jefferson, *Notes on the State of Virginia*, 1787.

Nor have we been wanting in attention to our British brethren. We have warned them from time to time of attempts by their legislature to extend a jurisdiction over these our states. We have reminded them of the circumstances of our emigration & settlement here, no one of which could warrant so strange a pretension: that these were effected at the expense of our own blood & treasure, unassisted by the wealth or the strength of Great Britain: that in constituting indeed our several forms of government, we had adopted one common king, thereby laying a foundation for perpetual league & amity with them: but that submission to their parliament was no part of our constitution, nor ever in idea, if history may be credited: and, we appealed to their native justice and magnanimity as well as to the ties of our common kindred to disavow these usurpations which were likely to interrupt our connection and correspondence. They too have been deaf to the voice of justice & of consanguinity, and when occasions have been given them, by the regular course of their laws, of removing from their councils the disturbers of our harmony, they have, by their free election, re-established them in power. At this very time too they are permitting their chief magistrate to send over not only soldiers of our common blood, but Scotch & foreign mercenaries to invade & destroy us. These facts have given the last stab to agonizing affection, and manly spirit bids us to renounce forever these unfeeling brethren. We must endeavor to forget our former love for them, and hold them as we hold the rest of mankind, enemies in war, in peace friends. We might have been a free and a great people together; but a communication of grandeur & of freedom it seems is below their dignity. Be it so, since they will have it. The road to happiness & to glory is open to us too. We will tread it apart from them, and acquiesce in the necessity which denounces our eternal separation!

Free and Independent

We therefore the representatives of the United States of America in General Congress assembled do in the name & by authority of the good people of these states reject & renounce all allegiance & subjection to the kings of Great Britain & all others who may hereafter claim by, through or under them: we utterly dissolve all political connection which may heretofore have subsisted between us & the people or parliament of Great Britain: & finally we do assert & declare these colonies to be free & independent states, & that as free & independent states, they have full power to levy war, conclude peace, contract alliances, establish commerce, & to do all other acts & things which independent states may of right do.

And for the support of this declaration we mutually pledge to each other our lives, our fortunes, & our sacred honor.

"A bill of rights is . . . necessary in the general constitution."

The Constitution Needs a Bill of Rights

Brutus

The US Constitution was written in 1787 and ratified on June 21, 1788. During the intervening months, a political party called the Anti-Federalists opposed the document. One of their complaints was that it had no bill of rights. The anonymous essays of Brutus, sometimes attributed to Robert Yates, an American political leader, were published in the *New York Journal* and addressed to the people of New York state to urge them not to ratify the proposed Constitution. In the following viewpoint, excerpted from the November 1, 1787, essay, the author argues that a bill of rights is necessary because liberty is not secure without a written guarantee.

As you read, consider the following questions:

1. According to the author, what caution should be observed when forming a constitution?
2. Why does the author want a bill of rights for the national constitution as well as for state constitutions?
3. Why should government be restricted, according to Brutus?

Brutus, "'To the Citizens of the State of New-York," *New York Journal*, November 1, 1787.

Though it should be admitted, that the argument[s] against reducing all the states into one consolidated government, are not sufficient fully to establish this point; yet they will, at least, justify this conclusion, that in forming a constitution for such a country, great care should be taken to limit and define its powers, adjust its parts, and guard against an abuse of authority. How far attention has been paid to these objects, shall be the subject of future enquiry. When a building is to be erected which is intended to stand for ages, the foundation should be firmly laid. The constitution proposed to your acceptance, is designed not for yourselves alone, but for generations yet unborn. The principles, therefore, upon which the social compact is founded, ought to have been clearly and precisely stated, and the most express and full declaration of rights to have been made—But on this subject there is almost an entire silence. . . .

The Security of the Nation

Those who have governed, have been found in all ages ever active to enlarge their powers and abridge the public liberty. This has induced the people in all countries, where any sense of freedom remained, to fix barriers against the encroachments of their rulers. The country from which we have derived our origin is an eminent example of this. Their magna charta and bill of rights have long been the boast, as well as the security, of that nation. I need say no more, I presume, to an American, than, that this principle is a fundamental one, in all the constitutions of our own states; there is not one of them but what is either founded on a declaration or bill of rights, or has certain express reservation of rights interwoven in the body of them. From this it appears, that at a time when the pulse of liberty beat high and when an appeal was made to the people to form constitutions for the government of themselves, it was their universal sense, that such declarations should make a part of their frames of government. It is therefore the more astonishing, that this grand security, to the rights of the people, is not to be found in this constitution.

It has been said, in answer to this objection, that such declaration[s] of rights, however requisite they might be in the constitutions of the states, are not necessary in the general constitution, because, "in the former case, every thing which is not reserved is given, but in the latter the reverse of the proposition prevails, and every thing which is not given is reserved." It requires but little attention to discover, that this mode of reasoning is rather specious than solid. The powers, rights, and authority, granted to the general government by this constitution, are as complete, with respect to every object to which they extend, as that of any state government—It reaches to every thing which concerns human happiness—Life, liberty, and property, are under its controul. There is the same reason, therefore, that the exercise of power, in this case, should be restrained within proper limits, as in that of the state governments. To set this matter in a clear light, permit me to instance some of the articles of the bills of rights of the individual states, and apply them to the case in question.

Securing Life and Liberty

For the security of life, in criminal prosecutions, the bills of rights of most of the states have declared, that no man shall be held to answer for a crime until he is made fully acquainted with the charge brought against him; he shall not be compelled to accuse, or furnish evidence against himself—The witnesses against him shall be brought face to face, and he shall be fully heard by himself or counsel. That it is essential to the security of life and liberty, that trial of facts be in the vicinity where they happen. Are not provisions of this kind as necessary in the general government, as in that of a particular state? The powers vested in the new Congress extend in many cases to life; they are authorised to provide for the punishment of a variety of capital crimes, and no restraint is laid upon them in its exercise, save only, that "the trial of all crimes, except in cases of impeachment, shall be by jury; and such trial shall be in the state where the said crimes shall have been committed." No man is secure of a trial in the county where he is charged to have committed a crime; he may be brought from Niagara to New-York, or carried from Kentucky to Richmond for trial for an offence, supposed to be committed. What security is there, that a man shall be furnished with a full and plain description of the charges against him? That he shall be allowed to produce all proof he can in his favor? That he shall see the witnesses against him face to face, or that he shall be fully heard in his own defence by himself or counsel?

Inestimable Value

A declaration of rights is of inestimable value. It contains those principles which the government never can invade without an open violation of the compact between them and the citizens.

Agrippa, VI, December 14, 1787.

For the security of liberty it has been declared, "that excessive bail should not be required, nor excessive fines imposed, nor cruel or unusual punishments inflicted—That all warrants, without oath or affirmation, to search suspected places, or seize any person, his papers or property, are grievous and oppressive."

These provisions are as necessary under the general government as under that of the individual states; for the power of the former is as complete to the purpose of requiring bail, imposing fines, inflicting punishments, granting search warrants, and seizing persons, papers, or property, in certain cases, as the other.

Securing Property

For the purpose of securing the property of the citizens, it is declared by all the states, "that in all controversies at law, respecting property, the ancient mode of trial by jury is one of the best securities of the rights of the people, and ought to remain sacred and inviolable."

Does not the same necessity exist of reserving this right, under this national compact, as in that of these states? Yet nothing is said respecting it. In the bills of rights of the states it is declared, that a well regulated militia is the proper and natural defence of a free government—That as standing armies in time of peace are dangerous, they are not to be kept up, and that the military should be kept under strict subordination to, and controuled by the civil power.

The same security is as necessary in this constitution, and much more so: for the general government will have the sole power to raise and to pay armies, and are under no controul in the exercise of it; yet nothing of this is to be found in this new system.

I might proceed to instance a number of other rights, which were as necessary to be reserved, such as, that elections should be free, that the liberty of the press should be held sacred; but the instances adduced, are sufficient to prove, that this argument is without foundation.—Besides, it is evident, that the reason here assigned was not the true one, why the framers of this constitution omitted a bill of rights; if it had been, they would not have made certain reservations, while they totally omitted others of more importance. We find they have, in the 9th section of the 1st article, declared, that the writ of habeas corpus shall not be suspended, unless in cases of rebellion—that no bill of attainder, or expost facto law, shall be passed—that no title of nobility shall be granted by the United States, &c. If every thing which is not given is reserved, what propriety is there in these exceptions? Does this constitution any where grant the power of suspending the habeas corpus, to make expost facto laws, pass bills of attainder, or grant titles of nobility? It certainly does not in express terms. The only answer that can be given is, that these are implied in the general powers granted. With equal truth it may be said, that all the powers, which the bills of right, guard against the abuse of, are contained or implied in the general ones granted by this constitution.

So far it is from being true, that a bill of rights is less necessary in the general constitution than in those of the states, the contrary is evidently the fact.—This system, if it is possible for the people of America to accede to it, will be an original compact: and being the last, will, in the nature of things, vacate every former agreement inconsistent with it. For it being a plan of government received and ratified by the whole people, all other forms, which are in existence at the time of its adoption, must yield to it. This is expressed in positive and unequivocal terms, in the 6th article, "That this constitution and the laws of the United States, which shall be made in pursuance thereof, and all treaties made, or which shall be made, under the authority of the United States, shall be the supreme law of the land; and the judges in every state shall be bound thereby, any thing in the *constitution*, or laws of any state, *to the contrary* notwithstanding.

"The senators and representatives before-mentioned, and the members of the several state legislatures, and all executive and judicial officers, both of the United States, and of the several states, shall be bound, by oath or affirmation, to support this constitution."

It is therefore not only necessarily implied thereby, but positively expressed, that the different state constitutions are repealed and entirely done away, so far as they are inconsistent with this, with the laws which shall be made in pursuance thereof, or with treaties made, or which shall be made, under the authority of the United States: of what avail will the constitutions of the respective states be to preserve the rights of its citizens? should they be plead, the answer would be, the constitution of the United States, and the laws made in pursuance thereof, is the supreme law, and all legislatures and judicial officers, whether of the general or state governments, are bound by oath to support it. No priviledge, reserved by the bills of rights, or secured by the state government, can limit the power granted by this, or restrain any laws made in pursuance of it. It stands therefore on its own bottom, and must receive a construction by itself without any reference to any other—And hence it was of the highest importance, that the most precise and express declarations and reservations of rights should have been made.

Restricting Government

This will appear the more necessary, when it is considered, that not only the constitution and laws made in pursuance thereof, but all treaties made, or which shall be made, under the authority of the United States, are the supreme law of the land, and supersede the constitutions of all the states. The power to make treaties, is vested in the president, by and with the advice and consent of two thirds of the senate. I do not find any limitation, or restriction, to the exercise of this power. The most important article in any constitution may therefore be repealed, even without a legislative act. Ought not a government, vested with such extensive and indefinite authority, to have been restricted by a declaration of rights? It certainly ought.

So clear a point is this, that I cannot help suspecting, that persons who attempt to persuade people, that such reservations were less necessary under this constitution than under those of the states, are willfully endeavouring to deceive, and to lead you into an absolute state of vassalage.

4

"Bills of rights . . . are not only unnecessary in the proposed Constitution, but would even be dangerous."

The Constitution Does Not Need a Bill of Rights

Publius

A political group known as the Federalists supported the Constitution as it was originally written in 1787 and urged the states to ratify it. Their views were defined in *The Federalist Papers*, written by Alexander Hamilton, John Jay, and James Madison. In the following viewpoint, excerpted from the eighty-fourth *Federalist Paper* and addressed to the people of New York state, the author argues that a bill of rights is unnecessary because the Constitution adequately protects civil liberties. The essays originally appeared with the general signature of Publius, but authorship of this one is attributed to Hamilton, the leader of the Federalist party.

As you read, consider the following questions:

1. What examples does the author give of rights secured by the original Constitution?
2. According to Publius, why were bills of rights originally needed?
3. Why might a bill of rights be dangerous, according to the author?

Publius, "On Alleged Defects in the Constitution," *The Federalist Papers*, 1788.

The most considerable of the remaining objections is that the plan of the Convention contains no bill of rights. Among other answers given to this, it has been upon different occasions remarked that the constitutions of several of the States are in a similar predicament. I add that New York is of the number; and yet the opposers of the new system in this State who profess an unlimited admiration for its Constitution, are among the most intemperate partisans of a bill of rights. To justify their zeal in this matter, they allege two things: one is that though the Constitution of New York has no bill of rights prefixed to it, yet it contains in the body of it various provisions in favor of particular privileges and rights, which, in substance, amount to the same thing; the other is that the Constitution adopts, in their full extent, the common and statute law of Great Britain, by which many other rights, not expressed in it, are equally secured.

To the first I answer that the Constitution proposed by the Convention contains, as well as the Constitution of this State, a number of such provisions.

Rights Secured by the Constitution

Independent of those which relate to the structure of the government, we find the following: Article I, section 3, clause 7, "Judgment in cases of impeachment shall not extend further than to removal from office, and disqualification to hold and enjoy any office of honor, trust, or profit under the United States; but the party convicted shall, nevertheless, be liable and subject to indictment, trial, judgment, and punishment according to law"; section 9 of the same article, clause 2, "The privilege of the writ of *habeas corpus* shall not be suspended, unless when in cases of rebellion or invasion the public safety may require it"; clause 3, "No bill of attainder or *ex post facto* law shall be passed"; clause 7, "No title of nobility shall be granted by the United States; and no person holding any office of profit or trust under them, shall, without the consent of the Congress, accept of any present, emolument, office, or title of any kind whatever, from any king, prince, or foreign State"; article 3, section 2, clause 3, "The trial of all crimes, except in cases of impeachment, shall be by jury; and such trial shall be held in the State where the said crimes shall have been committed; but when not committed within any State, the trial shall be at such place or places as the Congress may by law have directed"; section 3 of the same article, "Treason against the United States shall consist only in levying war against them, or in adhering to their enemies, giving them aid and comfort. No person shall be convicted of treason, unless on the testimony of two witnesses to the same overt act, or on confession in open court"; and clause 3 of the same section, "The Congress shall have power to declare the punishment of treason; but no attainder of treason

34

shall work corruption of blood, or forfeiture, except during the life of the person attainted.''

It may well be a question whether these are not, upon the whole, of equal importance with any which are to be found in the Constitution of this State. The establishment of the writ of *habeas corpus*, the prohibition of *ex post facto* laws, and of titles of nobility, to which we have no corresponding provisions in our Constitution, are, perhaps, greater securities to liberty and republicanism than any it contains. The creation of crimes after the commission of the fact, or, in other words, the subjecting of men to punishment for things which, when they were done, were breaches of no law, and the practice of arbitrary imprisonment, have been in all ages the favorite and most formidable instruments of tyranny. . . .

An Unessential Amendment

My own opinion has always been in favor of a bill of rights; provided it be so framed as not to imply powers not meant to be included in the enumeration. At the same time I have never thought the omission a material defect, nor been anxious to supply it even by *subsequent* amendment, for any other reason than that it is anxiously desired by others. . . .

I have not viewed it in an important light because I conceive that in a certain degree . . . the rights in question are reserved by the manner in which the federal powers are granted.

James Madison, letter to Thomas Jefferson, October 17, 1788.

To the second, that is, to the pretended establishment of the common and statute law by the Constitution, I answer that they are expressly made subject "to such alterations and provisions as the legislature shall from time to time make concerning the same." They are, therefore, at any moment liable to repeal by the ordinary legislative power, and, of course, have no constitutional sanction. The only use of the declaration was to recognize the ancient law, and to remove doubts which might have been occasioned by the Revolution. This consequently can be considered as no part of a declaration of rights; which under our constitutions must be intended as limitations of the power of the government itself.

Outdated Purpose

It has been several times truly remarked that bills of rights are, in their origin, stipulations between kings and their subjects, abridgments of prerogative in favor of privilege, reservations of rights not surrendered to the prince. Such was Magna Charta, obtained by the barons, sword in hand, from King John. Such were the subsequent confirmations of that charter by succeeding princes. Such was the Petition of Right assented to by Charles I, in the beginning of his reign. Such, also, was the Declaration of Right presented by the Lords and Commons to the Prince of Orange in 1688, and afterward thrown into the form of an act of Parliament called the Bill of Rights. It is evident, therefore, that, according to their primitive signification, they have no application to constitutions professedly founded upon the power of the people, and executed by their immediate representatives and servants. Here, in strictness, the people surrender nothing; and, as they retain everything, they have no need of particular reservations. "We, the people of the United States, to secure the blessings of liberty to ourselves and our posterity, do ordain and establish this Constitution for the United States of America." Here is a better recognition of popular rights than volumes of those aphorisms which make the principal figure in several of our State bills of rights, and which would sound much better in a treatise of ethics than in a constitution of government.

But a minute detail of particular rights is certainly far less applicable to a constitution like that under consideration, which is merely intended to regulate the general political interests of the nation, than to a constitution which has the regulation of every species of personal and private concerns. If, therefore, the loud clamors against the plan of the Convention on this score are well founded, no epithets of reprobation will be too strong for the Constitution of this State; but the truth is that both of them contain all which, in relation to their objects, is reasonably to be desired.

Unnecessary and Dangerous

I go further, and affirm that bills of rights, in the sense and to the extent in which they are contended for, are not only unnecessary in the proposed Constitution, but would even be dangerous. They would contain various exceptions to powers not granted, and on this very account would afford a colorable pretext to claim more than were granted; for why declare that things shall not be done which there is no power to do? Why, for instance, should it be said that the liberty of the press shall not be restrained, when no power is given by which restrictions may be imposed? I will not contend that such a provision would confer a regulating power, but it is evident that it would furnish, to men disposed to usurp, a plausible pretence for claiming that power. They might urge with a semblance of reason that the Constitution ought not to be charged with the absurdity of providing against the abuse of an authority which was not given, and that the provision against restraining the liberty of the press afforded a clear implication that a power to prescribe proper regulations concerning it was intended to be vested in the national government. This may serve as a specimen of the numerous handles which would be given to the doctrine of constructive powers by the indulgence of an injudicious zeal for bills of rights. . . .

Idle Distinctions

The constitution, or whole social compact, is but one instrument, no more or less, than a certain number of articles or stipulations agreed to by the people, whether it consists of articles, sections, chapters, bills of rights, or parts of any other denomination, cannot be material. Many needless observations, and idle distinctions, in my opinion, have been made respecting a bill of rights.

The Federal Farmer, XVI, January 20, 1788.

There remains but one other view of this matter to conclude the point. The truth is, after all the declamation we have heard, that the Constitution is itself, in every rational sense, and to every useful purpose, a bill of rights. The several bills of rights in Great Britain form its Constitution, and, conversely, the constitution of each State is its bill of rights; and the proposed Constitution, if adopted, will be the bill of rights of the Union. Is it one object of a bill of rights to declare and specify the political privileges of the citizens in the structure and administration of the government? This is done in the most ample and precise manner in the plan of the Convention; comprehending various precautions for the public security, which are not to be found in any of the State constitutions. Is another object of a bill of rights to define certain immunities and modes of proceeding, which are relative to personal and private concerns? This we have seen has also been attended to, in a variety of cases, in the same plan. Adverting, therefore, to the substantial meaning of a bill of rights, it is absurd to allege that it is not to be found in the work of the Convention. It may be said that it does not go far enough, though it will not be easy to make this appear; but it can with no propriety be contended that there is no such thing. It certainly must be immaterial what mode is observed as to the order of declaring the rights of the citizens, if they are to be found in any part of the instrument which establishes the government; and, hence, it must be apparent that much of what has been said on this subject rests merely on verbal and nominal distinctions, entirely foreign from the substance of the thing.

5

"To violate the law, is to . . . tear the character of . . . liberty."

Obedience to Law Will Preserve Liberty

Abraham Lincoln

Abraham Lincoln, sixteenth president of the United States, held local, state, and national offices through years of tension that finally culminated in the outbreak of the Civil War. Many of his political speeches stressed the importance of preserving liberty and freedom during such difficult times. The following viewpoint is excerpted from a speech delivered before the Young Men's Lyceum of Springfield, Illinois, on January 27, 1838, twenty-three years before Lincoln became president. In it, he calls on his listeners to resist violence. He argues that only obedience to the laws will preserve individual liberty.

As you read, consider the following questions:

1. Why, according to President Lincoln, is the danger to the country greater from within than from without?
2. What will protect the country from this internal danger, according to the author?
3. What does Lincoln suggest should be done in the case of bad laws?

Abraham Lincoln, "The Perpetuation of Our Political Institutions," an address before the Young Men's Lyceum of Springfield, Illinois on January 27, 1838.

In the great journal of things happening under the sun, we, the American People, find our account running, under date of the nineteenth century of the Christian era. We find ourselves in the peaceful possession, of the fairest portion of the earth, as regards extent of territory, fertility of soil, and salubrity of climate. We find ourselves under the government of a system of political institutions, conducing more essentially to the ends of civil and religious liberty, than any of which the history of former times tells us. We, when mounting the stage of existence, found ourselves the legal inheritors of these fundamental blessings. We toiled not in the acquirement or establishment of them—they are a legacy bequeathed us, by a *once* hardy, brave, and patriotic, but *now* lamented and departed race of ancestors. Theirs was the task (and nobly they performed it) to possess themselves, and through themselves, us, of this goodly land; and to uprear upon its hills and its valleys, a political edifice of liberty and equal rights; 'tis ours only, to transmit these, the former, unprofaned by the foot of an invader; the latter, undecayed by the lapse of time and untorn by usurpation, to the latest generation that fate shall permit the world to know. This task gratitude to our fathers, justice to ourselves, duty to posterity, and love for our species in general, all imperatively require us faithfully to perform.

How then shall we perform it? At what point shall we expect the approach of danger? By what means shall we fortify against it? Shall we expect some transatlantic military giant, to step the Ocean, and crush us at a blow? Never! All the armies of Europe, Asia and Africa combined, with all the treasure of the earth (our own excepted) in their military chest; with a Buonaparte for a commander, could not by force, take a drink from the Ohio, or make a track on the Blue Ridge, in a trial of a thousand years.

Danger from Among Us

At what point then is the approach of danger to be expected? I answer, if it ever reach us, it must spring up amongst us. It cannot come from abroad. If destruction be our lot, we must ourselves be its author and finisher. As a nation of freemen, we must live through all time, or die by suicide.

I hope I am over wary; but if I am not, there is, even now, something of ill-omen, amongst us. I mean the increasing disregard for law which pervades the country; the growing disposition to substitute the wild and furious passions, in lieu of the sober judgment of Courts; and the worse than savage mobs, for the executive ministers of justice. This disposition is awfully fearful in any community; and that it now exists in ours, though grating to our feelings to admit, it would be a violation of truth, and an insult to our intelligence, to deny. Accounts of outrages committed by mobs, form the every-day news of the times. They have pervaded the

A photograph by Alexander Hesler made in Springfield
on June 3, 1860.

country, from New England to Louisiana; they are neither peculiar
to the eternal snows of the former, nor the burning suns of the
latter; they are not the creature of climate—neither are they confined to the slave-holding, or the non-slave-holding States. Alike,
they spring up among the pleasure hunting masters of Southern
slaves, and the order-loving citizens of the land of steady habits.
Whatever, then, their cause may be, it is common to the whole
country. . . .

I know the American People are *much* attached to their Government; I know they would suffer *much* for its sake; I know they would endure evils long and patiently, before they would ever think of exchanging it for another. Yet, notwithstanding all this, if the laws be continually despised and disregarded, if their rights to be secure in their persons and property, are held by no better tenure than the caprice of a mob, the alienation of their affections from the Government is the natural consequence; and to that, sooner or later, it must come.

Here then, is one point at which danger may be expected.

The question recurs, "how shall we fortify against it?" The answer is simple. Let every American, every lover of liberty, every well wisher to his posterity, swear by the blood of the Revolution, never to violate in the least particular, the laws of the country; and never to tolerate their violation by others. As the patriots of seventy-six did to the support of the Declaration of Independence, so to the support of the Constitution and Laws, let every American pledge his life, his property, and his sacred honor; let every man remember that to violate the law, is to trample on the blood of his father, and to tear the character of his own, and his children's liberty. Let reverence for the laws, be breathed by every American mother, to the lisping babe, that prattles on her lap—let it be taught in schools, in seminaries, and in colleges; let it be written in Primers, spelling books, and in Almanacs;—let it be preached from the pulpit, proclaimed in legislative halls, and enforced in courts of justice. And, in short, let it become the *political religion* of the nation; and let the old and the young, the rich and the poor, the grave and the gay, of all sexes and tongues, and colors and conditions, sacrifice unceasingly upon its altars.

While ever a state of feeling, such as this, shall universally, or even, very generally prevail throughout the nation, vain will be every effort, and fruitless every attempt, to subvert our national freedom.

Obey Even Bad Laws

When I so pressingly urge a strict observance of all the laws, let me not be understood as saying there are no bad laws, nor that grievances may not arise, for the redress of which, no legal provisions have been made. I mean to say no such thing. But I do mean to say, that, although bad laws, if they exist, should be repealed as soon as possible, still while they continue in force, for the sake of example, they should be religiously observed. So also in unprovided cases. If such arise, let proper legal provisions be made for them with the least possible delay; but, till then, let them, if not too intolerable, be borne with.

6

"If it [the machine of government] . . . requires you to be the agent of injustice to another, then, I say, break the law."

Liberty Demands that Unjust Laws Be Broken

Henry David Thoreau

Henry David Thoreau, noted American author, championed individual freedom. In 1849 he refused to pay a poll tax because he believed it indirectly supported slavery. Consequently, he spent a night in prison. From that experience came his essay "On the Duty of Civil Disobedience," in which he stated that citizens should disobey unjust laws rather than tolerate the slightest reduction of their liberty. The essay has become a classic text in the timeless debate on civil liberties.

As you read, consider the following questions:

1. Why does Thoreau think that government is best which governs least?
2. On what should an individual base his or her actions, according to Thoreau?
3. What does Thoreau suggest should be done about unjust laws?

Henry David Thoreau, "On the Duty of Civil Disobedience." From *Walden: Or, Life in the Woods.* New York: Milestone Editions, 1854.

I heartily accept the motto,—"That government is best which governs least"; and I should like to see it acted up to more rapidly and systematically. Carried out, it finally amounts to this, which also I believe,—"That government is best which governs not at all"; and when men are prepared for it, that will be the kind of government which they will have. Government is at best but an expedient; but most governments are usually, and all governments are sometimes, inexpedient. The objections which have been brought against a standing army, and they are many and weighty, and deserve to prevail, may also at last be brought against a standing government. The standing army is only an arm of the standing government. The government itself, which is only the mode which the people have chosen to execute their will, is equally liable to be abused and perverted before the people can act through it. Witness the present Mexican war, the work of comparatively a few individuals using the standing government as their tool; for, in the outset, the people would not have consented to this measure.

This American government,—what is it but a tradition, though a recent one, endeavoring to transmit itself unimpaired to posterity, but each instant losing some of its integrity? It has not the vitality and force of a single living man; for a single man can bend it to his will. It is a sort of wooden gun to the people themselves. But it is not the less necessary for this; for the people must have some complicated machinery or other, and hear its din, to satisfy that idea of government which they have. . . .

Right Over Might

But, to speak practically and as a citizen, unlike those who call themselves no-government men, I ask for, not at once no government, but *at once* a better government. Let every man make known what kind of government would command his respect, and that will be one step toward obtaining it.

After all, the practical reason why, when the power is once in the hands of the people, a majority are permitted, and for a long period continue, to rule, is not because they are most likely to be in the right, nor because this seems fairest to the minority, but because they are physically the strongest. But a government in which the majority rule in all cases cannot be based on justice, even as far as men understand it. Can there not be a government in which majorities do not virtually decide right and wrong, but conscience?—in which majorities decide only those questions to which the rule of expediency is applicable? Must the citizen ever for a moment, or in the least degree, resign his conscience to the legislator? Why has every man a conscience, then? I think that we should be men first, and subjects afterward. It is not desirable to cultivate a respect for the law, so much as for the right. The only obligation which I have a right to assume, is to do at any time what I think right. It is truly enough said, that a corporation has no conscience; but a corporation of conscientious men is a corporation *with* a conscience. Law never made men a whit more just; and, by means of their respect for it, even the well-disposed are daily made the agents of injustice. . . .

Disobey Unjust Laws

Unjust laws exist; shall we be content to obey them, or shall we endeavor to amend them, and obey them until we have succeeded, or shall we transgress them at once? Men generally, under such a government as this, think that they ought to wait until they have persuaded the majority to alter them. They think that, if they should resist, the remedy would be worse than the evil. But it is the fault of the government itself that the remedy *is* worse than the evil. *It* makes it worse. Why is it not more apt to anticipate and provide for reform? Why does it not cherish its wise minority? Why does it cry and resist before it is hurt? Why does it not encourage its citizens to be on the alert to point out its faults, and *do* better than it would have them? Why does it always crucify Christ, and excommunicate Copernicus and Luther, and pronounce Washington and Franklin rebels?

A Higher Obligation

A strict observance of the written laws is doubtless *one* of the high duties of a good citizen, but it is not *the highest*. The laws of necessity, of self-preservation, of saving our country when in danger, are of higher obligation. To lose our country by a scrupulous adherence to written law, would be to lose the law itself, with life, liberty, property and all those who are enjoying them with us; thus absurdly sacrificing the end to the means.

Thomas Jefferson, letter to John B. Colvin, September 20, 1810.

One would think, that a deliberate and practical denial of its authority, was the only offense never contemplated by government; else, why has it not assigned its definite, its suitable and proportionate penalty? If a man who has no property refuses but once to earn nine shillings for the State, he is put in prison for a period unlimited by any law that I know, and determined only by the discretion of those who placed him there; but if he should steal ninety times nine shillings from the State, he is soon permitted to go at large again.

If the injustice is part of the necessary friction of the machine of government, let it go, let it go; perchance it will wear smooth,— certainly the machine will wear out. If the injustice has a spring, or a pulley, or a rope, or a crank, exclusively for itself, then perhaps you may consider whether the remedy will not be worse than the evil; but if it is of such a nature that it requires you to be the agent of injustice to another, then, I say, break the law. Let your life be a counter friction to stop the machine. What I have to do is to see, at any rate, that I do not lend myself to the wrong which I condemn.

As for adopting the ways which the State has provided for remedying the evil, I know not of such ways. They take too much time, and a man's life will be gone. I have other affairs to attend to. I came into this world, not chiefly to make this a good place to live in, but to live in it, be it good or bad. A man has not everything to do, but something; and because he cannot do *everything*, it is not necessary that he should do *something* wrong. It is not my business to be petitioning the Governor or the Legislature any more than it is theirs to petition me; and, if they should not hear my petition, what should I do then? But in this case the State has provided no way; its very Constitution is the evil. This may seem to be harsh and stubborn and unconciliatory; but it is to treat with the utmost kindness and consideration the only spirit that can appreciate or deserve it. So is all change for the better, like birth and death which convulse the body. . . .

Toward Respect for the Individual

The authority of government, even such as I am willing to submit to,—for I will cheerfully obey those who know and can do better than I, and in many things even those who neither know nor can do so well,—is still an impure one: to be strictly just, it must have the sanction and consent of the governed. It can have no pure right over my person and property but what I concede to it. The progress from an absolute to a limited monarchy, from a limited monarchy to a democracy, is a progress toward a true respect for the individual. Even the Chinese philosopher was wise enough to regard the individual as the basis of the empire. Is a democracy, such as we know it, the last improvement possible in government? Is it not possible to take a step further towards recognizing and organizing the rights of man? There will never be a really free and enlightened State, until the State comes to recognize the individual as a higher and independent power, from which all its own power and authority are derived, and treats him accordingly. I please myself with imagining a State at last which can afford to be just to all men, and to treat the individual with respect as a neighbor; which even would not think it inconsistent with its own repose, if a few were to live aloof from it, not meddling with it, nor embraced by it, who fulfilled all the duties of neighbors and fellow-men. A State which bore this kind of fruit, and suffered it to drop off as fast as it ripened, would prepare the way for a still more perfect and glorious State, which also I have imagined, but not yet anywhere seen.

Understanding Words in Context

Readers occasionally come across words which they do not recognize. And frequently, because they do not know a word or words, they will not fully understand the passage being read. Obviously, the reader can look up an unfamiliar word in a dictionary. However, by carefully examining the word in the context in which it is used, the word's meaning can often be determined. A careful reader may find clues to the meaning of the word in surrounding words, ideas, and attitudes.

Below are sentences adapted from the viewpoints in this chapter. In each excerpt, one or two words are printed in italics. Try to determine the meaning of each word by reading the excerpt. Under each excerpt you will find four definitions for the italicized word. Choose the one that is closest to your understanding of the word.

Finally, use a dictionary to see how well you have understood the words in context. It will be helpful to discuss with others the clues which helped you decide on each word's meaning.

1. The Constitution of the United States is the supreme law of the land, and thus *SUPERSEDES* the constitutions of the states.

   SUPERSEDES means:
   a) experiences   c) remains under
   b) comes before   d) negates

2. A common and natural result of an undue respect for law is, for example, a soldier marching against his will and conscience. Such a man is a mere shadow, a *REMINISCENCE* of humanity, a faint echo of a time when he was free.

   REMINISCENCE means:
   a) remembrance
   b) exact copy
   c) rebirth
   d) exaggeration

3. Take, for example, the lynching of the man in St. Louis. He had *FORFEITED* his life, by committing an outrageous murder; and had he not been lynched, he would have been soon sentenced to death by the law.

   FORFEITED means:
   a) won
   b) corrected
   c) fulfilled
   d) lost

4. When I urge a strict observance of all the laws, let me not be understood to say there are no bad laws, nor that complaints may not arise, for the *REDRESS* of which, no law has been made. But, there is no complaint that is a fit object of *REDRESS* by mob law.

   REDRESS means:
   a) setting right
   b) law
   c) clothe again
   d) loss

5. Rulers have been found in all times who are eager to enlarge their powers and take away the public liberty. This has led the people in all countries, who still have a proper sense of freedom, to put up barriers against the *ENCROACHMENTS* of their rulers.

   ENCROACHMENTS means:
   a) crimes
   b) speeches
   c) gradual intrusions
   d) gifts

6. Government is at best but an *EXPEDIENT*; but most governments become an obstacle to freedom. The government itself, which is only the mode which the people have to do their will, is liable to be abused and perverted.

   EXPEDIENT means:
   a) experience
   b) illusion
   c) means to an end
   d) oppressive act

Should the Church and the State Remain Separate?

Chapter Preface

The First Amendment to the US Constitution begins: "Congress shall make no law respecting an establishment of religion, or prohibiting the free exercise thereof." With these words, the writers of the Constitution made clear their intention that church and state remain separate; that government shall not meddle in the affairs of religion, and religion shall not meddle in the affairs of state. How absolute that separation should be and how it is best maintained, however, have been a matter of debate since the amendment was ratified in 1791.

The question of separation is complicated. Some people interpret the First Amendment as a strict and uncrossable line. They believe that government should not support activities that could be interpreted as religious, such as prayer in schools or nativity scenes on public property. Other people believe such separation is a gross exaggeration of the First Amendment's original intent. They interpret the First Amendment as a protection against government sponsorship of *a particular* religion, not as a censure against all religions. These people believe that prayer in schools or nativity scenes at Christmas merely reflect America's religious heritage.

The debates in this chapter cover areas in which the First Amendment is constantly being tested. They demonstrate that legislation on everything from taxes to school clubs can become a battleground for government and religious groups if people begin to feel that their religious liberties are threatened.

"For government to intrude itself into religious practices constitutes a clear and present danger."

Church and State Must Remain Separate

Samuel Rabinove

Samuel Rabinove is the legal director of The American Jewish Committee. The following viewpoint is excerpted from a speech he delivered at a symposium on church-state relations at Southern Baptist Theological Seminary in Louisville, Kentucky. In it, Rabinove acknowledges that religion has powerfully influenced American culture and politics, but he insists that matters of state and matters of religion should remain separate. If government intervenes in religion, Rabinove states, Americans may lose their religious freedom.

As you read, consider the following questions:

1. According to Rabinove, what relationship between the church and the state did the writers of the Constitution intend? How did he determine what they intended?
2. How does the author show that church and state are no longer separate? Who does he blame for this erosion?
3. Why is Rabinove upset by any government involvement in religion?

Samuel Rabinove, "Religious Liberty and Church-State Separation: Why Should We Care?" a speech delivered at Southern Baptist Theological Seminary, Louisville, Kentucky on April 10, 1986.

Of all the religious sects in the early days of America, there is no question that the Baptists were the most impassioned in the fight for religious freedom and separation of church and state. John Leland, a prominent Baptist minister, wrote in 1820, "The liberty I contend for is more than toleration. The very idea of toleration is despicable; it supposes that some have a pre-eminence above the rest to grant indulgence; whereas *all* should be equally free, Jews, Turks (Moslems), Pagans and Christians. Test oaths and established creeds should be avoided as the worst of evils."

The fight for religious freedom, as we know, was neither an easy one, nor a short one. Jews in Maryland, for example, were not permitted to hold public office until 1825, and in North Carolina, not until 1868. And, in 1843 in New York City, a group of Jewish parents whose children attended public schools, where religion was part of the normal curriculum, protested the content of a textbook called *American Popular Lessons.* The Board of Education appointed a committee to look into the matter. The report of this committee, which rejected the Jewish protest, read in part as follows: "Our committee has examined the several passages and lessons alluded to, and they are unable to discover any possible ground of objection, even by the Jews, except what may arise from the fact that they are chiefly derived from the New Testament and inculcate the general principles of Christianity." Well, what can one say? That kind of insensitivity has its present-day counterpart in the attitude of many sincere, well-intentioned Christians who cannot understand why Jewish parents object to devotional Christmas observances in public schools.

Original Intentions

It is often said . . . that America is predominantly a Christian country, and therefore, this sort of thing is to be expected. Yet in the Constitution of the United States, of course, there is no mention of Jesus Christ. . . . Nowhere in the original Constitution was there any mention either of Jesus or of God the Creator. Since many, if not most, of the Founding Fathers were God-fearing Christians, these omissions scarcely could have been inadvertent. They knew very well what they were doing, and not doing.

Jefferson and Madison were painfully aware of what had happened to heretics, dissenters and infidels of all denominations in country after country in Europe where church and state had been joined. They knew too that our country was settled in large part by refugees from such religio-political despotisms (Puritans, Quakers, Mennonites, Catholics, Lutherans, Huguenots, Baptists, Jews and many others) some of whom, ironically, were themselves infected with the virus of intolerance and were prepared to deny to others in America the very freedom of worship which they so passionately had demanded for themselves in Europe. The

Anglicans, for example, drove the Puritans out of England; shortly thereafter, the Puritans drove the Baptists out of the Massachusetts Bay Colony. Subsequently, Roger Williams founded in Rhode Island, not only the first Baptist church in America, but also the first American colony to rigorously separate church and state and to grant total religious freedom to all its inhabitants. Not surprisingly, Rhode Island soon became a haven for Jews.

A major factor in the development of freedom of conscience in America was a paper issued by James Madison in 1785. In his "Memorial and Remonstrance against Religious Assessments," Madison contended that support of religion should be voluntary, that taxation to subsidize religion would create enmity and would endanger freedom. This paper was most influential in shaping the First Amendment. . . .

Religious Pluralism

There is no question whatever that religious and spiritual values have contributed immeasurably to human progress from barbarism to civilization. The United States, certainly, has been profoundly influenced for the better by Judeo-Christian moral and ethical values. Unlike countries with established churches, however, many religions have thrived in pluralistic America, hand-in-hand with our longstanding tradition of separation of church and state, which has served as a bulwark of religious liberty for all. (In Sweden, for example, with its established Lutheran Church, attendance at religious worship is far less than in the United States. In Norway, also with an established Lutheran Church, Jesuits were actually barred by the Constitution from entering the country until the Constitution was amended in 1956.) . . .

Maintaining a High Wall

The First Amendment has erected a wall between church and state. That wall must be kept high and impregnable. We could not approve the slightest breach.

Justice Hugo Black, *Everson v. Board of Education,* 1947.

It is precisely the constitutionally mandated principle of separation of church and state that has guaranteed all Americans in our pluralistic society the freedom to join or not join any denomination, and, despite certain shameful episodes involving dissident sects (the Mormons, for example, who were driven as far west as Utah by mob violence), diverse religions have flourished here with a vitality and a minimum of divisiveness that are the envy of religious men and women the world over. (For dramatic contrast, consider northern Ireland today.) The separation principle has also allowed non-believers, so many of whom are no less moral or decent or patriotic than people of faith, to live as equal citizens without penalty or stigma.

Alexis de Tocqueville, writing of his travels in America in 1830, said this:

> The religious atmosphere of the country was the first thing that struck me on arrival in the United States. . . .
>
> My longing to understand the reason for this phenomenon increased daily.
>
> To find this out, I questioned the faithful of all communions; I particularly sought the society of clergymen, who are the depositaries of the various creeds and have a personal interest in their survival . . . all thought the main reason for the quiet sway of religion over their country was the complete separation of church and state. I have no hesitation in stating that throughout my stay in America I met nobody, lay or cleric, who did not agree about that.

A Tradition of Separation

Those who are inclined today to rebuke the "separationist" Justices on the U.S. Supreme Court as being outside the American tradition (as the religious New Right and certain leading members of the Reagan Administration are fond of doing), would do well to note the views enunciated by the Supreme Court during the last century. In *Melvin v. Easley* (1860), the Court declared, "Christianity is not established by law, and the genius of our institutions requires that the Church and the State should be kept separate. . . . The state confesses its incompetency to judge spiritual matters between men or between man and his maker . . . spiritual matters are exclusively in the hands of the teachers of religion." And, in *Darwin v. Beason* (1890), the Court affirmed that "the First Amendment of the Constitution . . . was intended to allow everyone under the jurisdiction of the United States to entertain such notions respecting his relation to his maker, and the duties they impose, as may be approved by his conscience, and to exhibit his sentiments in such form of worship as he may think proper, not injurious to the rights of others, and to prohibit legislation for the support of any religious tenets, or the modes of worship of any sect."

As noted by my good friend, Dr. James E. Wood, Jr., editor of the *Journal of Church and State*, marginal religions have contributed significantly to our understanding of religious pluralism, as well as to judician interpretations of religious liberty, far out of proportion to their numerical membership. Consider, for example, Jehovah's Witnesses, who probably have been responsible for more cases dealing with religious liberty than any other single sect. In the Jehovah's Witness "flag salute" case of *West Virginia Board of Education v. Barnett*, in 1943, the Court squarely addressed the constitutional guarantee of religious pluralism: "If there is any fixed star in our constitutional constellation, it is that no official, high or petty, can prescribe what shall be orthodox in politics, nationalism, religion, or other matters of opinion or force citizens to confess by word or act their faith therein. If there are any circumstances which permit any exception, they do not occur to us." In a more recent marginal religion case, the American Jewish Committee joined with Christian groups, including the American Baptist Churches, in a challenge to a charitable solicitation ordinance in Clearwater, Florida, aimed specifically at the Church of Scientology, which would affect all of us adversely, if it were upheld.

Keep Church and State Separate

If any provision of the Constitution can be said to be more precious than the others, it is the provision of the First Amendment which undertakes to separate church and state by keeping government's hands out of religion and by denying to any and all religious denominations any advantage from getting control of public policy or the public purse.

This is so because the history of nations makes this truth manifest: When religion controls government, political freedom dies; and when government controls religion, religious freedom perishes.

Sam J. Ervin Jr., *Church & State*, February 1985.

The Supreme Court in 1947, in another of its periodic attacks of logic and principle, in the case of *Everson v. Board of Education*, enunciated a rule of law, which was subscribed to by the entire bench at the time and reaffirmed in subsequent cases, in the following terms: "'The establishment of religion' clause of the First Amendment means at least this: Neither state nor federal government can set up a church. Neither can pass laws which aid one religion, aid all religions, or prefer one religion over another. . . . No tax in any amount, large or small, can be levied to support any religious activities or institutions, whatever they may be called, or whatever form they may adopt to teach or practice religion. Neither a state nor the federal government can, openly or secretly, participate in the affairs of any religious organizations or groups and *vice-versa*. In the words of Jefferson, the clause against establishment of religion by law was intended to erect 'a wall of separation between church and state.'" As many of us will recall, Jefferson's words came from his famous letter in 1802 to the Danbury, Connecticut Baptist Association: "Believing with you that religion is a matter which lies solely between Man and his God . . . I contemplate with sovereign reverence that act of the whole American people which declared that their legislature should 'make no law respecting an establishment of religion, or prohibiting the free exercise thereof,' thus building a wall of separation between church and state."

In any event, the Supreme Court and the First Amendment notwithstanding, there has never been in this country total separation of church and state. Actually, there have been quite a few accommodations between church and state in America—including government aid to religion such as military chaplaincies, tax exemption for religious property used for religious purposes, and tax deductibility of contributions to churches and synagogues—which are widely accepted as reasonable and proper. There are other issues of church-state separation, however, which have been in sharp dispute and where the question often is: Where shall an intelligent line be drawn? . . .

Erosion of the Separation Principle

Sad to relate, there has been a serious erosion of commitment by the executive branch to the separation principle. A U.S. ambassador has been appointed to the Vatican, which is essentially an ecclesiastical entity, its role as a state notwithstanding. And Secretary of Education William J. Bennett said that two U.S. Supreme Court rulings (*Grand Rapids School District v. Ball; Aquilar v. Felton*), which barred public school systems from sending their teachers at public expense into parochial schools to teach remedial and enrichment classes, were a "ridiculous" expression of the Court's "fastidious disdain for religion that is hard to fathom." The Justice Department had filed briefs on the side of government aid to religious schools in both cases. The American Jewish Committee joined with the Baptist Joint Committee on Public Affairs and the National Council of Churches in the *Grand Rapids* case, on the opposite side. We maintained that it is not the business of government to subsidize schools whose chief reason for being is to propagate a religious faith—any faith, including our own. Mr. Bennett said that these rulings would not deter the Reagan Administration from persisting in its efforts to enact legislation providing for tuition tax credits or vouchers for parents of pupils in religious schools.

Even the U.S. Supreme Court, in some of its recent decisions, seemingly has moved toward accommodation of religion by government, as in the Pawtucket, Rhode Island case of *Lynch v. Donnelly* where, in 1984, the Court upheld (5-4) the constitutionality of a city-owned, city funded and city-sponsored Nativity scene, as part of a larger annual Christmas display. . . .

When the Solicitor General of the United States, in response to a question from Supreme Court Justice John Paul Stevens during the oral argument in the Pawtucket creche case, replied that, in his opinion, it would not be unconstitutional for a city to use public funds to celebrate Mass (provided nobody is *forced* to attend), something is gravely amiss. This is not "conservative." Rather it represents a radical departure from American tradition. If the principle of separation of church and state is to have substance in America, it should mean at least this: the state must not behave as if it were a church, or a synagogue. Nor may it serve as an agent for any religion. The state must not do for citizens things which, in their rightful free exercise of religion, they are perfectly capable of doing for themselves. For government to intrude itself into religious practices (such as school prayer), or to seek to impose particular religious beliefs or values on citizens who do not share them (such as prohibition of abortion), constitutes a clear and present danger to Americans of all faiths. In sum, the state must be neutral, not partisan, in matters religious, even when neutrality may be painful to some. For example, the American Jewish Committee filed a brief *amicus* in the U.S. Supreme Court, jointly with the Christian Legal Society and the Lutheran Church-Missouri Synod upholding the right of the Dayton Christian Schools, a fundamentalist group, to dismiss a woman teacher because of the school's sincere religious conviction that a mother of an infant should remain home to care for her infant, in spite of the Ohio civil rights law against sex discrimination. The First Amendment, we believe, forbids government to dictate the employment practices of religious schools.

In a major speech in New York City, Sen. Edward Kennedy of Massachusetts said eloquently what needed to be said.

> There is a long and unhappy history of intolerance which still flourishes at the extreme fringe of American politics. . . . But today that extremist tradition also infects the very center of our national authority. We have a President who has announced that those who disagree with him on officially prescribed school prayer or nationally proscribed abortion are "intolerant of religion"—that they are somehow or other anti-God or anti-truth. . . . What *is* the proper relationship between church and state, between religious values and national decisions? . . . Religious leaders may say anything they feel bound in conscience to say, but they may not ask Government to do something which it cannot do under the Constitution or the social contract of a pluralistic society. . . . In cases like abortion or prayer or sexual identity—the proper role of religion is to appeal to the free conscience of each person, not the coercive rule of secular law. . . .

"It is not only impossible but not necessary to separate religion totally from society."

Separation of Church and State Is Unnecessary

Martin R. Tripole

Martin R. Tripole teaches theology at St. Joseph's University in Philadelphia, Pennsylvania. In the following viewpoint, he states that liberals have pushed the separation of church and state to an extreme. According to Tripole, the writers of the Constitution never intended to completely divorce religion from government. He concludes that strict separation of church and state disrupts the natural relationship between society and religion.

As you read, consider the following questions:

1. What are the two religion clauses in the First Amendment? How does the author paraphrase them?
2. According to Tripole, why is total separation of religion from other areas of life impossible?
3. What two assertions does Tripole make about the First Amendment? How does he support those assertions?

Martin R. Tripole, "Religion and the First Amendment: How the Supreme Court Has Misinterpreted the Constitution," *Crisis*, June 1987. Excerpted with permission from *Crisis* magazine, PO Box 1006, Notre Dame, IN 46556.

That God is being removed more and more from the public forum is not simply a matter of chance. It is part of the secularization process going on in our society. While this process has been underway at least since the dawn of the modern era, it is being especially abetted today by a philosophical and legal viewpoint widespread in American society, that religion should by definition be separated from society, and must be so separated in view of the demands of the First Amendment of the Constitution of the United States.

If both of these positions were true, we should have a serious obstacle to maintaining a transcendent dimension to our lives in the world. But are they true? . . . It is appropriate to look at these questions. Inasmuch as the answers to them have so much importance in determining the quality of life in America, as well as our ability to experience the presence of the transcendent, they are worth investigating carefully.

Should Religion Be Separated from Society?

The question is a curious one, since we do not make a point of separating other areas of life, such as politics, business, and the arts. Why religion? Moreover, even if we tried to isolate these areas of thought and life from the operations of society, it would not be possible to do so, for our lives are not made up of separately defined areas. What is impossible regarding other areas of life is impossible also regarding religion.

Since total separation is unrealistic and impossible, should not "limits" be placed upon the influence of each of these areas, preserving their individual identity while preventing them from infringing upon each other or overwhelming the operations of society? But if this is the better alternative, then our position might be stated this way: it is not only impossible but not necessary to separate religion totally from society, although it would be desirable to control the operations of religion so that it retains its own identity and does not engulf other areas.

Let's carry our argument one step further. It is not even desirable to try to extricate religion from society; if we do so, the public operations of society inevitably lose their transcendent dimension. Without a transcendent dimension to social life, people are unable to see the relevance of faith to their larger lives; faith becomes an optional superstructure in the public forum. As a result, people inevitably begin to explain reality as a matter of course without a relationship to God, and the structures of society take on a nonatheistic, and finally an atheistic, configuration. Divorced from its proper relationship to God in the order of creation, the public order does not simply remain neutral to God; it necessarily takes on a configuration of its own in opposition to its divinely-created origins. This leads to atheism, in practice if not in theory.

To argue for a religious dimension to life in society within proper limits is not necessarily to argue for the involvement of the Church as such in the affairs of the state as such. Theoretically, one might be in favor of the former but be opposed to the latter, for in the latter case we are talking about two distinct institutions having distinct interests, operations, and goals.

Widespread among Americans today is the notion that the First Amendment legislates "separation of church and state." Yet many do not even know that the words "separation of church and state" are nowhere found in the Constitution, or that it is hotly disputed on the Supreme Court whether the Constitution mandates such a separation, even though the majority on the Court in recent years has so ruled. Also disputed is whether the Court's understanding of the church-state relationship remains faithful to what the Framers of the First Amendment *intended*. The question is whether the Court has so interpreted the document as to oppose the intentions of the Framers, and to be in fundamental violation of the human rights granted by the Constitution. We need, therefore, to be clear about what the First Amendment does in fact say. . . .

No Wall Intended

The Founding Fathers never intended to establish an absolute wall between church and state. The framers only intended, as Justice William H. Rehnquist put it in a Supreme Court dissent, "to prohibit the designation of any church as a 'national' one [and] to stop the Federal Government from asserting a preference for one religious denomination or sect over others."

Rosemarie Zagarri, *The New Republic*, September 9, 1985.

The Amendment asserts: "Congress shall make no law respecting the establishment of religion, or prohibiting the free exercise thereof." The Establishment Clause holds that Congress shall not legally establish religion in this country; the Free Exercise Clause, that Congress shall do nothing to prevent people from freely exercising their religious convictions. Both statements are deceptively simple; their precise meaning has become a subject of much controversy in recent history, as a result of the Supreme Court's efforts to rule authoritatively on their meaning. The clauses do involve some ambiguity, and the Founders themselves are not here to provide clarification. They formulated the amendment, however, within the framework of their views on life and the problems they faced. We may, therefore, legitimately draw upon their other writings, as well as on our understanding of the world in which they lived, to aid in the resolution of those ambiguities. . . .

Two questions are apt regarding the Establishment Clause: (1)

Does it forbid legally favoring religion over non-religion, or only the legal establishment of a specific religion? and (2) Does it refer simply to the obligations of the federal government or to those of the states as well?

The Supreme Court has in recent years asserted that

- the clause forbids both favoring religion over irreligion and the establishment of one specific religion over another; and that
- this prohibition must be understood as applying (through the Fourteenth Amendment) to the states as well.

Americans tend to give an almost "sacred," indisputable authority to the highest court, much as Catholics traditionally do to the Pope and to Vatican decisions. Yet the Supreme Court possesses no "infallibility." The possibility of error clearly arises when one realizes how closely its decisions are often made, many of which, on religious questions, have been decided by a 5-4 vote. Further, considerable disagreement with the Court's decisions on religious matters exists among legal and constitutional scholars.

I submit that (1) the amendment addresses only the national government and asserts that Congress shall make no law establishing a *national* religion (though the Fourteenth Amendment may have extended this prohibition later to the states as well); and (2) the amendment addresses only the establishment of a *specific* religion and not religion as such. It therefore intends that Congress shall make no law establishing one religion rather than another as the national religion. It does not address the matter of religion as opposed to irreligion. . . .

No Need for Neutrality

The Framers of the First Amendment wanted to ensure there would be no national establishment of a particular religion, while never intending that the federal government should be neutral toward religion altogether. Indeed, Chief Justice William Rehnquist reminds us that none of the members of the First Congress who debated and ratified the First Amendment

expressed the slightest indication that they thought the language before them from the Select Committee, or the evil to be aimed at, would require that the Government be absolutely neutral as between religion and irreligion. The evil to be aimed at, so far as those who spoke were concerned, appears to have been establishment of a national church, and perhaps the preference of one religious sect over another; but it was definitely not concern about whether the Government might aid all religions evenhandedly.

More likely, it was taken for granted by the Framers that in denying a preferred status to any one religion, the government would be benevolent toward all religions. In the years during and after the enactment of the First Amendment the First Congress and several presidents undertook such benevolent practices toward religion. Congress enacted "a day of public thanksgiving and prayer" and presidents Washington, (John) Adams, and Madison issued Thanksgiving proclamations calling for such a day from 1789 to 1815. Washington's first "National Thanksgiving Proclamation" states that Thursday, November 26, 1789 "be devoted by the people of these States to the service of that great and glorious Being who is the beneficent author of all the good that was, and is, or will be," and that they render him "our sincere and humble thanks for His kind care," and that they pray to "the great Lord and Ruler of Nations . . . to promote the knowledge and practice of true religion and virtue" everywhere. Congress also continued to supply government monies for the needs of specific religious groups, Catholic and Protestant, either for education or for the spreading of the Gospel. . . .

Defining Separation

In what way, more specifically, does the Establishment Clause separate church and state? Many constitutional scholars argue that the Fourteenth Amendment (ratified in 1868) extended the First Amendment to the individual states as well. If so, it follows that the Bill of Rights forbids on the state level exactly what it forbids on the national level, and no more.

Government Should Support Religious Activities

What the ACLU and Americans United do not see are the second and third principles we have enunciated: that total withdrawal of government from religion denies the religious rights of many Americans; and that some of their most treasured values as American citizens are reached more effectively through religious instruction and religious persuasion than by any other means. Our citizens would be poorer citizens, our government would be less desirable, our society would be impoverished were it not for such religious activity. Government should do this not to further a particular religion, or even religion in general. But it should encourage and indeed support such religious activities in its own self-interest, for the highest good of its citizens. For government to refuse such services only on the ground that they will indirectly support traditional religion amounts to an antireligious bias—a bias directly contrary to the Constitution.

Kenneth S. Kantzer, *Christianity Today,* April 8, 1983.

In *Everson* v. *Board of Education* (1947) the Supreme Court drew up a comprehensive definition of the separation of church and state that went far beyond the above. The Court now asserted a "high and impregnable . . . wall of separation between church and state," citing these last words from Thomas Jefferson to substantiate a policy of rigid exclusion of national as well as state governments from *any* activities which might aid religion or religious activities and institutions.

There are serious problems with this decision. While Jefferson indeed said those words, he did so in the context of a letter to the Danbury Baptists in 1802, eleven years after the debate on, and ratification of, the First Amendment. (Jefferson did not take part in the debate, being out of the country at the time.) He certainly did not intend his phrase to have reference to state government, whose religious rights were not under scrutiny. Authority regarding religious affairs, including the relationship of religion to education, was in the hands of the states. In the words of Robert Cord, Jefferson could only have meant the "wall of separation . . . in regard to possible federal action such as a law establishing a national religion or prohibiting the free exercise of worship [since] Congress had no other power in religious matters to curb." Further, if we assume that Jefferson had intended a greater separation, we are then unable to explain how as president he could have enacted policies which allocated public monies to religious groups—the Roman Catholic Church in one case, the Society of the United Brethren in Pennsylvania in another—for educational and religious activities.

Misinterpretations

The fact is that the Supreme Court in 1947 misinterpreted Jefferson's words to have far greater meaning than he had intended. The Court in *Everson* went so far as to assert that the "wall of separation" meant

> at least this: Neither a state nor the Federal Government can set up a church. Neither can pass laws which aid one religion, aid all religions, or prefer one religion over another. . . . No tax in any amount, large or small, can be levied to support any religious activities or institutions, whatever they may be called, or whatever form they may adopt to teach or practice religion. Neither a state nor the Federal Government can, openly or secretly, participate in the affairs of any religious organizations or groups and *vise versa*.

Few of the above statements are justifiable interpretations of the First Amendment or of principles operative in earlier American history. The first statement is accurate, as we have shown. The second is accurate, except for the clause "aid all religions." Herein lies the Court's major deviation from the meaning of the First Amendment. As Cord points out, "There is no historical evidence to suggest, however, that the Establishment Clause in any way constitutionally precludes non-discriminatory governmental aid to religion. In fact, the converse is confirmed historically." As to the third and fourth sentences, Cord states:

> Did not the prayers of Congressional Chaplains in the First
> Congress, which formed the Establishment Clause, constitute
> "religious activities"? Were their salaries not paid from tax
> revenues? Are not these same activities, performed in the U.S.
> Congress for clergymen today, irreconcilable with the Court's
> interpretation? How can the clear and direct financial aid to mis-
> sionaries and the U.S. treaties to build Churches [in the late eigh-
> teenth and nineteenth centuries] be reconciled with the *Ever-*
> *son* definition?

A Religious Society

The doctrine of strict separation flies in the face of a social reality
that remains persistently, stubbornly religious. The unending turmoil engendered by the Supreme Court decision on prayer in the
public schools is the best example of this collision: whatever may
have been the careful legal reasoning behind the decision, the fact
remains that millions of Americans have perceived it as a solemn
declaration that, their most dearly held beliefs and values having
been disavowed by the highest authority of the Republic, their country has become officially godless.

Peter L. Berger, *Commentary*, May 1986.

Unfortunately, the Court continued to base its decisions on the
error of historical interpretation made in *Everson*. Thus in 1948
the majority ruled that public school property could not be used
for religious instruction, since this constituted state "aid" to
religion. In 1962 the Court held that the Establishment Clause prohibited authorizing prayer in public schools, even when the prayer
was nondenominational. In 1963 the Court prohibited reading the
Lord's Prayer or a passage from the Bible at the opening of school,
even though participation was voluntary, and once again firmly
committed itself to neutrality regarding religion. In 1982 the Court
upheld a ruling that Louisiana's law allowing voluntary prayer sessions in public schools was unconstitutional. In 1985 it issued
several rulings antagonistic to religion: Connecticut's law giving
employees a right to a day free from work on their chosen Sab-
bath was declared unconstitutional; "shared time" and community
education programs providing classes to nonpublic school students
at public expense in classrooms located in and leased from the
nonpublic schools were held to be unconstitutional; New York City's use of federal funds received under the Elementary and Secondary Education Act of 1965 (a program which had endured for
twenty years without problems) to pay salaries of public school
employees to teach educationally deprived children from low-
income families in parochial schools was declared unconstitu-

tional; and a 1981 Alabama law authorizing a one-minute period of silence in all public schools "for meditation or voluntary prayer" was held to be unconstitutional because the law was motivated for the purpose of advancing religion.

On the other hand, there have been rulings which have tended to favor religion, although the Court justified them on the basis that they did not. For example: the 1984 ruling allowing taxpayers' money for the display of nativity scenes at Christmas; the 1981 ruling that when a state university allows its facilities to be used by student organizations, religious groups must be included; the 1983 ruling that a Minnesota law which permits parents to claim state tax deductions for children's school expenses, even if they attend nonpublic schools, is constitutional; and the 1983 ruling validating the use of paid chaplains in state legislatures and in the houses of Congress. Though it is difficult to decipher how such rulings do not favor religion, the Supreme Court justified each of them *only* because it interpreted them as not doing so, thus (at least in its own eyes) standing by its continuing norm of neutrality toward religion.

Failure of the Three-Part Formula

The Court has constructed a three-part formula by which it tests most laws regarding the state's relationship to religion: "First, the statute must have a secular legislative purpose; second, its principal or primary effect must be one that neither advances nor inhibits religion . . . ; finally, the statute must not foster 'an excessive government entanglement with religion'" (*Lemon* v. *Kurtzman*). Justice William Brennan has more recently added a fourth criterion, that the given statute not create "a serious potential for divisive conflict over the issue of aid to religion."

As a result of this complicated formula the Court has created serious problems for itself. It has ended up insisting upon a "wall of separation" between church and state, but not an "absolute" one; it permits state statutes that do not foster "excessive" involvement in religious matters. The Court deliberately did not want to make the separation absolute, because such a separation is deemed not only undesirable, but impossible to enact. But then the question becomes how to determine this "fine line" of separation.

The Court has had an extremely difficult time trying to apply its three (or four) part formula. Chief Justice Rehnquist has pointed out the extremely circuitous and conflicting route the Court has taken in trying to measure up to these complicated criteria, which have caused it to end with "hopelessly divided pluralities." Its "historically faulty doctrine" has "proven all but useless as a guide to sound constitutional adjudication" and "should be frankly and explicitly abandoned."

"The First Amendment limits what public schools can do on matters of religion, not what students can do."

Schools Should Allow Religious Activity

Nat Hentoff

Nat Hentoff, a well-known civil libertarian, writes a monthly column for *The Progressive*. In the following viewpoint, he supports the Equal Access Law which allows public school students to gather on campus for any kind of activity, including religious activity. According to Hentoff, permitting religious group meetings preserves freedom of religion and freedom of expression. He states that students benefit from the diversity of views offered by a variety of religious and political groups.

As you read, consider the following questions:

1. According to Hentoff, what distinction is being forgotten in the dispute over religious activity in schools?
2. What experience with high school students has the author had? How has that experience shaped his opinion of the Equal Access Law?
3. Why does Hentoff favor a diversity of religious and political groups on high school campuses?

Nat Hentoff, "Who's First on the Fourth," *The Progressive*, December 1984. Copyright © 1984, The Progressive, Inc. Reprinted by permission from The Progressive, Madison, WI 53703.

To many liberals, including many civil libertarians, there is no place for religion in the public schools. Not only does the First Amendment forbid prayer in the classroom or auditorium, they say, but *any* form of religious speech is so dangerous to impressionable students that the schoolhouse door must be barred to all such speech.

For example, a chapter of the American Civil Liberties Union in the state of Washington threatened to sue a public school district because a high school was about to stage the rock opera, *Jesus Christ, Superstar*. Showing that vivid work, said the ACLU chapter, is an act of "religious instruction" that "has no place in a public school." Presumably, that ACLU chapter would also ban Beethoven's *Missa Solemnis* and John Coltrane's *A Love Supreme* for fear that those works might turn students on to some god or other.

Letting in Religion

A case in the Federal courts underscores the fear that many school boards and principals have of letting a wisp of religion slip into their schools. In Minnesota, a high school senior asked permission to distribute a religious newspaper in school. He was turned down on the basis of a state board of education rule that "public schools may not be used for the religious socialization of students" and, accordingly, must not allow the distribution of Bibles or religious tracts.

The Minnesota student decided to engage in civil disobedience on First Amendment grounds, and he distributed the paper. He pointed out that when the school authorities tried to impose a prior restraint on him, "they broke the First Amendment three times— freedom of speech, freedom of the press, and freedom of religion." The authorities suspended him.

In this instance, the ACLU affiliate did not flinch at the word "religion." The Minnesota chapter is supporting the young man. And in an editorial, the *Minneapolis Star and Tribune* gave the principal and the school board a much-needed refresher course in the First Amendment: "The First Amendment limits what public schools can do on matters of religion, not what students can do—at least within the bounds of nondisruptive behavior. The distinction is the difference between upholding the First Amendment and violating it."

The Equal Access Law

Those who believe religion has an "insinuating" influence on the young—whether initiated by students or not—don't recognize the distinction between what students can do and what the state cannot do. A tumultuous case in point is the Federal Equal Access bill that was passed and signed into law [in 1984]. Under the statute, any public school receiving Federal funds that allows voluntary student groups to meet before or after regular school hours must also permit religious clubs to assemble. All clubs must be student-initiated, without a trace of sponsorship by the school or by any teacher. Furthermore, the legislation requires that all student clubs, including religious ones, be subject to the school's authority to maintain order and to make sure that "attendance of students at meetings is voluntary."

With the Reverend Sun Myung Moon and other pied pipers in mind, the Equal Access law also warns that "non-school persons may not direct, conduct, control, or regularly attend activities of student groups." And to maintain order, a school can decide that certain "non-school persons" can't come in.

Don Meredith, reprinted with permission.

The bill was initially introduced to open public schools to student religious clubs, but when that didn't pass muster in Congress, a compromise was reached to prohibit discrimination—in the words of the statute—"against any students who wish to conduct a meeting . . . on the basis of the religious, political, philosophical, or other content of the speech at such meetings."

This means, for instance, that a nuclear freeze club—formerly banned at some schools for being too "political"—now has the right to meet. Even the ACLU, whose national board generally regards any religious speech in school as gnawing away at the Bill of Rights, found some good in the Equal Access measure. It didn't support the bill because of its fears that the student religious clubs may turn into recruitment agencies. But the ACLU didn't oppose the bill, either: "The statute is a serious student rights initiative," said Barry Lynn of the Washington, D.C., office. "It would be of real benefit to many political and other student groups which seek ACLU assistance."

Opposition

Groups fiercely devoted to separation of church and state fought the bill, however, until the very moment of the final vote. Seymour Reich, head of the National Civil Rights Committee of the Anti-Defamation League of B'nai B'rith, argued that "peer influence and conformity are strongest during the high school years. One can easily imagine the pressure students will feel (or exert) to join (or involve) friends in their religious club, disregarding their own religious beliefs."

Opponents of the bill charged that Equal Access was "an unconstitutional attempt to put prayer back into the public schools," and that members of minority faiths would be coerced into religious exercises.

"This will mark the first time in our history," said Representative Don Edwards of California, the most impassioned defender of the Bill of Rights in the House, "in which Federal law will license and encourage religious services in our schools. Under any definition, this is Government sponsorship of religion."

Another opponent, Senator Howard Metzenbaum of Ohio, said, "I do not understand why anyone would want to force our schools to give bizarre cults access to our teen-agers."

A Vote for Equal Access

Yet a staunch civil libertarian, Representative Barney Frank of Massachusetts, voted for Equal Access, and his reasons for doing so are worth repeating: "There are friends of mine whom I respect greatly who say that somehow we ought never to allow religious-oriented activities to take place on public property, particularly with regard to schools. I think that is in error," he explained on the House floor. "I think that the coercive aspect of school prayers led by teachers is wrong, undercuts fundamental freedoms, and ought not to be allowed, but wholly voluntary activities where outsiders can be prevented from coming in, as under this bill, after school, initiated by students themselves, whether for religious, political, or philosophical purposes, seems to me legitimate.

"Indeed, Mr. Speaker, I regard this as a very auspicious day in many ways in regard to those of us who think we ought not to infantilize teen-agers. This is a bill which recognizes the rights of teen-agers in the high schools to say that if any group is allowed to meet, then all groups—so long as they do not break either the laws or the furniture—should be allowed to meet in the school buildings. It is . . . an empowering of teen-agers so that the school boards and the school authorities can no longer pick and choose for these teen-agers. They can no longer say, 'If you have a meeting of this club, you can't have of a meeting of that one.'

"It is a piece of legislation which says that if we are going to allow access to the schools for the Young Republicans and the Young Democrats, then all political opinions are going to be let in. . . . It is non-coercive. . . . I do not see any damage that comes to the fabric of this society from the fact that some teen-agers might decide to have a meeting of a radical political group while others might decide to have a meeting of a particular religious society. I think those of us who think teen-agers ought to be treated with some respect for their individuality ought to welcome this bill."

Against Religion

But the failure to incorporate religion in some way into the intellectual pageantry of education is an act of aggression against religion, and a kind of wartime mobilization of all that is secular, against all that is religious. If Congress is expected to bow its head once a day, and the President of the United States to swear fidelity with his hand on the Bible, how is it that contact with religion, however fleeting, should not be expected in the schools?

William F. Buckley Jr., *Manchester Union Leader,* March 15, 1984.

But that is precisely the point. Much of the opposition to Equal Access came from those who do not believe teen-agers are individuals yet—at least not to the degree that they can withstand peer pressure.

I spend a fair amount of time with high school students when I am invited by teachers or by students who have read my history of the First Amendment or various articles I've written on censorship and the like. In every school I've worked in, from Boulder to Brooklyn, I have seen more disinclination toward conformity among students than among many of the adults I know. Once they grasp what the Bill of Rights is all about, teen-agers get quite excited. (Most of this material is new to them because our liberties are so ineptly taught in the schools.) They get excited because they are able to stretch their polemical skills in arguing with their peers about privacy, free press and speech, and the separation of church and state.

As Barney Frank says, many adults, including liberals and civil libertarians, do tend to infantilize teen-agers. So do most high school principals and many teachers. And that explains why one of the pervasive criticisms of American education in recent years has been the charge that students have not learned how to *think*—how to analyze what they've ingested. No wonder various cults have been successful in scooping up young people with little practice in critical thinking.

The presence of a diversity of religious and political groups—before and after school hours—can't help but stimulate students to think for themselves. Of course, some cults will try to proselytize, but they will then run into counter-arguments from other students who have become accustomed to intellectual dispute on these matters. (Now the process of conversion takes place under insulated, carefully controlled conditions.) In the light and heat of free-speech wars, the cults can be expected to wither away.

Thinking for Themselves

The degree to which high school students are capable of independent inquiry can be ascertained from "The Constitutional Dimensions of Student-Initiated Religious Activity in Public High Schools," an article in *The Yale Law Journal*, which points out that civil libertarians embrace a contradiction if they believe that high school kids aren't intellectually or emotionally mature enough to resist religious temptation, even if the source of that temptation is other students and not the school.

Opponents of religious activity argue that a student won't understand that the school is not *endorsing* a religious club by allowing it to meet. The concept of the school neutrally accommodating a voluntary student religious club is supposedly too subtle for immature teen-agers. Accepting this theory, most courts have ruled against student-initiated religious speech in high schools, and many civil libertarians applaud those courts.

On the other hand, however, civil libertarians and almost all courts have agreed . . . that students are intellectually and emotionally mature enough to run their own newspapers without school interference, unless the principal can prove that the students have printed material that is legally defamatory, obscene, or likely to cause a riot. If, in their school papers, teen-agers have the maturity to handle such complicated issues as birth control, draft registration, and national politics, then why can't they also be trusted to tell the difference between school sponsorship of religion and school accommodation of student-initiated religious speech? That is the basic contradiction many civil libertarians try to ignore.

Problems in the Court

In any case, the Equal Access bill, which does trust students to think for themselves, was signed by the President on August 11, [1984]. But this legislative remedy will have problems in the courts, for it is in conflict with a growing number of state and

Federal judicial decisions. The facts vary in each case, but the majority of the judges have felt that allowing even voluntary student religious groups to meet in public schools violates the clause of the First Amendment that prohibits government establishment of religion.

The lower-court decisions usually point to the Supreme Court's ruling in a case concerning equal access to student religious speech in a public university (*Widmar* v. *Vincent*, 1981). The Court, by an 8-to-1 vote, found that since the University of Missouri at Kansas City allowed other voluntary student groups to meet, it had established "a First Amendment forum" and therefore must also permit a club composed of evangelical Christians to use facilities on campus.

After all, said the Court, "an open forum in a public university does not confer any imprimatur of state approval on religious sects or practices. As the court of appeals quite aptly states, such a policy 'would no more commit the University . . . to religious goals,' than it is 'now committed to the goals of Students for a Democratic Society, the Young Socialist Alliance, or any other group eligible to use its facilities.'"

But—and this is the caveat that lower courts tend to underline in high school religious speech cases—the Supreme Court added: "University students are, of course, young adults. They are less impressionable than younger students and should be able to appreciate that the University policy is one of neutrality to religion.". . .

Exposure to All Ideas

One of the dissenting judges in a student religious speech case supported the teen-agers' position by quoting from a 1972 New York decision affirming a teacher's right to wear an armband in class to protest the war in Vietnam: "It would be foolhardy to shield our children from political debate and issues until the eve of their first venture into the voting booth. Schools must play an essential role in preparing their students to think and analyze and to recognize the demagogue."

Students do not need to be protected from ideas. For their intellectual and emotional well-being, they need to be exposed to all ideas, including those that speak of and for religion.

"There is serious doubt whether organized religious activities in public schools can ever be accomplished without impermissible state support."

Schools Should Not Allow Religious Activity

Norman Redlich

Editor and author Norman Redlich is the dean and a professor of law at New York University School of Law. His articles have appeared in journals such as *Journal of Legal Education, The Nation,* and *New York University Law Review.* In the following viewpoint, he condemns the Equal Access Law which allows religious activities in public schools. Redlich supports the separationist view that public schools are government property and thus should not allow prayer or religious meetings.

As you read, consider the following questions:

1. Why are issues of religious freedom and government involvement so confusing, according to Redlich?
2. According to the author, when is religious activity on public property constitutional? Why doesn't this condition apply to religious activity in schools?
3. What distinctions does Redlich draw between university and high school students?

Norman Redlich, "Religion and Schools: The New Political Establishment," in *Religion and the State: Essays in Honor of Leo Pfeffer,* ed. James E. Wood, Jr. Waco, TX: Baylor University Press, 1985. Reprinted with permission.

In the area of church-state relations, political pressures have been most intense, coming not only from evangelical groups like the Moral Majority, but also from a broad spectrum of Americans who sincerely believe that religion should play a greater role in this society and who look to government to support that view. Some believe that religious exercises are desirable in public schools; others seek financial relief from the heavy burden of private religious education for their children. They do not consider these positions as a threat to anyone's religious freedom. Indeed, living in a country with more religious freedom and diversity than any nation on earth, proponents of government aid to religion can easily overlook the crucial link between those freedoms and their constitutional source. As so often occurs with those who propound a religious message (usually their own), opposition to governmental support is often confused with opposition to religion itself. Sympathizers depict proponents of governmental aid as being on the side of God and religion, while the opponents are easily characterized as atheistic proponents of secular humanism. In such a political atmosphere, the rational defense of constitutional principles becomes increasingly difficult, and religious freedom and diversity are seriously threatened. Not surprisingly, the constitutional principle that forms the first line of defense is the one specifically designed for times such as these—the principle that church and state are best served by separation rather than by fusion.

The Supreme Court, despite the unpopularity of many of its decisions, has repeatedly reaffirmed its adherence to the concept of separation of church and state, even in its opinions upholding one form of tax assistance for private school tuition, the hiring of chaplains by legislatures, and the use of public funds for the construction of a nativity scene as part of a city's Christmas celebration. These decisions, however, are cause for serious concern. Regardless of the limitations expressed by the Court, they will be viewed by many as creating new opportunities for governmental endorsement of religious beliefs and institutions. In both courtroom and legislature, more pressure on the wall of separation can be expected.

The School Prayer Controversy

Nowhere has this assault on constitutional principles been more intense than in the controversy over school prayer. In 1962, in *Engel* v. *Vitale*, the Supreme Court held invalid a so-called nondenominational New York State Regents prayer. The eight-to-one decision, written by Justice Hugo Black, did not ban prayers in public schools. Individual children or teachers remain free to pray, as presumably many do for exams, or at the start of the day, or at occasions where individual conscience compels such observance. In this case, and in a similar case involving Bible reading one year later, the Court did hold invalid a state-sponsored religious observance that inevitably stamped the imprimatur of the state in support of religion. Such state support of religion, especially in the public schools, posed all of the dangers that the religion clauses of the Constitution were designed to avoid. Prayers could never be "neutral" among religions. No single prayer could satisfy all religious beliefs, thus leading to controversy among religions as to the nature of the prayer to be recited. The selection of any one prayer would throw the power of the state behind a particular set of religious beliefs and behind religion as against nonreligion. Edmond Cahn, a profoundly religious man and a constitutional scholar, pointed out at the time that the so-called nondenominational prayer in *Engel* v. *Vitale* was theologically offensive to many religious faiths. A government-supported religious exercise is inevitably coercive toward those who, for reasons of personal conviction, elect not to participate.

A Highly Suspect Act

In the light of the Supreme Court's familiar three-pronged test in judging the constitutionality of any legislation with respect to the Establishment Clause—a "secular legislative purpose," a "primary effect that neither advances nor inhibits religion," and the avoidance of "excessive government entanglement with religion"—the Equal Access Act should be viewed as highly suspect. From the beginning, the basic purpose of the bill was to require schools to permit students to hold religious meetings in public school facilities. The concept of "equal access" was seen as a secular means of accomplishing a religious purpose. There can be little question but that the desired and potential effect of equal access is seen by its proponents as the advancement of religion.

James E. Wood, *Religion & Public Education*, Summer 1985.

Thus, *Engel* v. *Vitale* did not break entirely new ground, although the controversy it generated created the impression that the Court had departed from, rather than followed, long-standing constitutional principles. A series of cases in the 1940s and 1950s had established the principle that the Establishment Clause of the First Amendment was intended not merely to prevent the creation of a state religion, as some proponents of state support for religion had argued, but rather to prevent state support for *all* religions as well as any particular religion. These Court decisions, dealing with the use of school facilities for religious instruction or with the reimbursement to parents for bus transportation to religious schools, had traced the historical origins of the Establishment Clause and concluded that separation of church and state, and not merely avoidance of state religion or the requirement that all religions be treated alike, was the guiding principle of interpretation of the Establishment Clause. Indeed, the decision of a sharply divided Court in *Everson* v. *Board of Education*, which upheld government reimbursement for bus transportation to parochial schools, was based on the Court's conclusion that such expenditures were not in support of religion but rather a kind of safety-and-welfare measure designed to help children travel to school without having to run the risk of walking along crowded highways.

Welfare or Aid to Religion?

Of course, as *Everson* indicated, there could be strong disagreement about whether a government program was an impermissible aid to religion or a general welfare measure, such as police and fire protection, where the exclusion of religious institutions would itself raise serious problems under the Free Exercise Clause. The bus transportation case demonstrated that the line was not always easy to discern since the Court agreed on the constitutional principle but divided five to four on the application. Similarly, differences could arise as to whether a practice or exercise, such as the singing of Christmas carols or the placing of Christmas trees in a public area, was religious or secular. A prayer read in school assemblies or in each class at the start of the day was clearly a religious exercise, as was the devotional reading of excerpts from the Bible, or the recitation of the Lord's Prayer, held unconstitutional in the *Schempp* case, decided one year after *Engel*.

In the prayer cases, the Court started to evolve its three-part test in evaluating whether a government practice violates the Establishment Clause. The practice must have a secular purpose; its principal or primary effect must neither advance nor inhibit religion; and it must not foster an excessive government entanglement with religion. A challenged practice must pass all three tests to be valid. State-sponsored prayer in the public schools fails all three.

The Underlying Principle of Separation

In the more than two decades since the school prayer cases were decided, there has been an almost unbroken line of court decisions applying the principles of these cases to a wide range of practices in different factual contexts. Clearly religious practices, such as a cross in the county seal, the placing of the Ten Commandments in classrooms, or the placing of a cross or other religious symbol in a public area, have been held to be establishments. The singing of Christmas songs, the objective teaching of religion, the study of the Bible as literature, and the exemption from the reach of Sunday closing laws for those whose religion requires Saturday observance have been held constitutional, and, in some instances, a desirable accommodation to protect the free-exercise claims of certain minorities. None of these cases has called into question the underlying principles enunciated in the school prayer cases of the early 1960s. . . .

[An] attempt to reintroduce a form of state-supported prayer in the public schools derives from the misguided reliance on that provision of the First Amendment that guarantees freedom of speech and the free exercise of religion. That schoolchildren have a right to pray is unquestioned. The Court has held that children cannot be compelled to salute the flag or recite the Pledge of Allegiance if such observances violate the student's religious beliefs. Permitting students to be excused, on religious grounds, from an otherwise secular observance is not an establishment of religion. Rather, it is a necessary accommodation by the state to the individual's religious freedom.

The Supreme Court Consensus

The historical consensus by the Supreme Court is that equal rights of conscience can best be served by the public schools' refraining from promoting such religious activities as Bible reading and prayers.

R. Freeman Butts, *Education Week*, February 2, 1983.

There are . . . situations where government interference with religious activity on public property would be unconstitutional. For example, if the public is permitted to gather at a park or at a facility such as the Mall in Washington, D.C., groups of individuals may not be prevented from similarly assembling if their purpose is to join in prayer. The principle is that once the state creates a public forum, it may not deny the use of that forum to religious groups, providing the state does not extend funds for a religious observance, as was the case with a visit by the pope to Philadelphia. Indeed, in *Widmar* v. *Vincent*, the Supreme Court held that if a state university makes its campus available for meetings by political and social groups, the university could not deny access to student religious groups even if such groups engage in religious worship. Thus, there will be occasions where religious exercises on public property are not only permissible, but are compelled by the Free Exercise Clause of the Constitution.

Some proponents of school prayer have sought to build on these decisions by requiring school officials to set aside time during the day to permit students in the public schools to organize groups for religious purposes, including engaging in prayer. One could argue that permitting student-initiated prayer clubs to meet during a school's "student-activity" period may not constitute an establishment of religion, and may, indeed, be required as an exercise of the student's rights to free speech and free exercise of religion. It is more likely, however, that setting aside time during each school day for student-initiated prayer constitutes the placing of an imprimatur of the state behind a religious exercise. By July 1984, all four federal courts of appeal that had considered the issue held varying forms of equal access to be unconstitutional. These courts distinguished *Widmar*, finding that unlike a university campus or a public park, where a wide variety of individuals and groups meet to express divergent views on political, and possibly religious, issues, a public secondary school has few of the characteristics of a public forum. Moreover, the process by which such student meetings or prayer sessions are organized could easily involve the type of official support that the school prayer cases sought to prevent. For example, this kind of official support was found by the court in *Lubbock*, where the policy on religious meetings in schools was part of an official statement setting forth guidelines for religion in the schools, and not part of a policy relating to free speech or student groups generally.

The Clamor for Equal Access

As these appeals courts reached unanimity regarding the unconstitutionality of allowing student religious groups and prayer clubs to meet on public school premises on school time, however, the public clamor over school prayer led Congress to seek a legislative solution to the problem. The proposals that were introduced were appealingly phrased in free-speech "equal access" terms and they required that all public schools that generally permit student groups to meet shall not discriminate against any group on the basis of the religious content of the speech at the meeting.

In May 1984, the House rejected an equal access bill that would have denied federal funds to school districts that refused to allow its high school students to hold religious meetings during noninstructional time on school premises. The final Senate version eliminated a number of the features that had made the earlier House draft so unappealing. It eliminated the cutoff of federal funds from noncomplying school districts, the virtually unlimited access to these student groups by outsiders and the bar to equal access for student religious groups that did not meet a numerical threshold. More importantly, however, the language of the Senate bill was broadened to extend protection not only to religious, but also to political, philosophical, and other speech at student meetings. This made the legislation more palatable to a variety of groups that had energetically opposed the earlier House version, and the Equal Access Act was overwhelmingly approved, both by many who had fought against President Reagan's proposed school prayer amendment and by many civil libertarians who

78

sincerely believe that the bill will serve the interests of student free speech.

There are, however, serious problems with this legislative solution. The constitutionality of the Equal Access Act is questionable, and the educational policy behind the desire to transform the high school into a public forum is misguided. The Equal Access Act requires secondary schools to do what *Widmar* requires of state universities, ignoring the fact that the principles of the *Widmar* case are not of universal applicability, even in the state university setting. Many valid distinctions may be drawn between the state university students in *Widmar* and the secondary students affected by Equal Access. High school students are younger and are likely to be more sensitive to suggestions by their school officials, even to suggestions that they participate in religious activities. Thus, there is serious doubt whether organized religious activities in public schools can ever be accomplished without impermissible state support. This is the essential teaching of the *McCollum* case. Unlike their university counterparts, high school students are subject to mandatory attendance requirements, and their educational programs are strictly controlled. High schools have traditionally not been open to all forms of collective speech and activity, but, rather, only to those programs that local school officials believe to be educationally sound. A high school is not London's Hyde Park. Finally, it is necessary to remember that the doctrine of the separation of government and religion stems not from hostility to religion or discrimination against it, but rather from a recognition that only a clear separation between the two is adequate to protect both the state and church from domination by the other.

"Taxing church property and income would destroy the free exercise of religion that the Bill of Rights seeks to protect."

Taxing Church Property Would Violate Civil Liberties

Jeffery Warren Scott

Most private property in the United States is taxed by the government. Churches, however, do not have to pay property taxes. In the following viewpoint, Jeffery Warren Scott supports this exemption and states that taxing church property would violate the First Amendment. Scott is assistant pastor of Grace Temple Baptist Church in Waco, Texas.

As you read, consider the following questions:

1. Why is the author concerned that churches will lose their tax-exempt status?
2. According to Scott, how does tax exemption differ from subsidies?
3. What reasons does the author give for maintaining tax exemptions for churches?

In 1977 the chief counsel of the Baptist Joint Committee on Public Affairs, the late John Baker, warned of a coming crisis for the church over the issue of property taxation. Because a growing population was placing increasing demands on the government for public services, Baker was convinced that government would begin to look for additional sources of revenue, and that church property would be a prime target for taxation.

What was clear to Baker in 1977 is even more obvious [a decade later]. Government obligations and deficits have continued to escalate, pushing the federal debt ceiling higher and higher. The Reagan administration has responded to the crisis by trying to shift many social programs down to the state level. The result has been—and will continue to be—an enormous burden on states' already strained budgets.

The potential impact of this shift on churches becomes apparent when one realizes that the average local government receives 64 per cent of its general revenue from property taxes and that churches own a vast amount of untaxed property. In 1976, one study estimated that church property was worth at least $118 billion. In times of budget difficulty, it is only natural that churches will be considered for taxation.

To be sure, state and local government budgets have been strained before with little threat to churches' tax-exempt status. This time, however, courts have made it possible to remove the property tax exemption currently enjoyed by the churches. To understand the courts dramatic shift it is necessary to understand the history of the exemption.

The History of Tax Exemption

The notion of tax exemption for church property is an old one. Genesis 47:26 records Pharaoh exempting the priests' land from taxation, and Ezra 7:24 indicates that none of the priests, Levites, singers, porters or ministers of the house of God were to be charged tax, toll or custom. In the days of Roman Emperor Constantine, church buildings and the land surrounding them were exempt. Centuries later, European countries continued the tradition of exemption, albeit because the church frequently controlled the state.

In the U.S., property tax exemption for churches began in colonial days and continued with the birth of the new nation. In 1802, for instance, the Seventh Congress specifically exempted religious bodies from real estate taxes. On the state level, specific exemptions from property taxes for churches were established in Virginia in 1777, New York in 1799, and the city of Washington in 1802. "The exemptions [for churches] have continued uninterrupted to the present day," Justice William J. Brennan has said. "They are in force in all 50 states."

Despite this long and unbroken history of property tax exemption for churches in this country, courts have recently paved the way for the destruction of this privilege, by setting precedents that can easily be used to end all church property tax exemption.

The Walz Case

The Supreme Court's shift away from the time-honored position of tax exemption first became apparent in 1970 when the court handed down its opinion in *Walz v. Tax Commission of the City of New York*. Walz had sued to enjoin the New York City Tax Commission from granting property tax exemption to religious organizations for properties used solely for religious worship. He argues that the exemptions indirectly required him to make a contribution to religious bodies and thereby violated the establishment clause of the First Amendment. In a close 5-4 decision, the court held that exempting church property was permissible, but not constitutionally required.

A Preferred Position

In the United States, it has been a basic public policy since the founding of the nation to accord to freedom of religion, speech, press and assembly a "preferred position" at the head of the Bill of Rights. Christians support and affirm this healthful arrangement of the civil order, not solely or primarily for themselves and their churches, but for everyone. . . . Society is stronger and richer for the voluntary associations in which citizens voluntarily band together for constructive purposes independent of government support and therefore of government control. Exemption from taxation is one way in which government can and does foster such voluntary groups.

The National Council of Churches, in *Religion and the State*, 1985.

Many church groups filed *amicus curiae* briefs urging that the court declare a constitutional requirement of property tax exemption for churches. However, the court sidestepped this question, preferring to focus instead on the establishment clause. The court reasoned that property tax exemption differed from a tax subsidy—which would be impermissible under the entanglement principle of the free-exercise clause—because:

the government does not transfer part of its revenue to churches but simply abstains from demanding that the church support the state. . . . There is no genuine nexus between tax exemption and establishment of religion.

Had the court ruled that the tax exemption was a subsidy, there is little doubt that the 5-4 decision would have been reversed and the exemption declared unconstitutional.

In 1972 the federal courts began making the same shift. In *Chris-*

tian Echoes National Ministry, Inc. v. U.S., the Tenth Circuit Court addressed what the *Walz* decision had sidestepped, and held that "tax exemption is a privilege, a matter of grace rather than a right."

A Dangerous Shift

The major shift of the Supreme Court came in 1983 when, in *Regan v. Taxation with Representation*, the court held . . . that tax exemption was equivalent to a tax subsidy. The question before the court involved tax exemption for nonprofit organizations—religious, charitable, scientific, public-safety-oriented, literary or educational. Justice William H. Rehnquist spoke for the court:

> Both tax exemptions and tax deductibility are a form of subsidy that is administered through the tax system. A tax exemption has much the same effect as a cash grant to the organization of the amount of tax it would have to pay on its income.

The significance of this decision is often overlooked. If tax exemption is a form of subsidy, then church property tax exemption is a clear violation of the establishment clause of the First Amendment. All that is necessary to make church property tax exemption a thing of the past is for an irate taxpayer who is tired of high taxes to file suit to force churches to pay their "fair share." With the *Regan v. Taxation* precedent in effect, the court could easily slip from the 5-4 *Walz v. Tax Commission* position and rule property tax exemption for religious institutions to be unconstitutional.

Another omen of the impending ill is found in the *Bob Jones University v. U.S.* decision, which was issued the day after *Regan v. Taxation*. In *Bob Jones*, the Court declared that religious schools that are tax-exempt or that receive tax-deductible contributions must comply with government policy or lose their tax-deductible status. Bob Jones University had been following religiously motivated practices that had the effect of discriminating against blacks. The Court upheld the Internal Revenue Service's decision to withdraw the university's right to receive tax-deductible contributions because discrimination was contrary to public policy.

The danger of the *Bob Jones* decision is that if the university can be forced to comply with public policy in order to retain its tax status, then all other nonprofit institutions—with churches listed first in the tax regulation—can be forced to do likewise. The logical end of the *Bob Jones* decision would be to take away the tax-exempt status of churches that actively oppose U.S. military involvement in Central America, that speak out against current policy on nuclear weapons, or that provide sanctuary to aliens in violation of Immigration and Naturalization Service policy.

When *Regan v. Taxation* is linked with *Bob Jones*, the Court's direction on the question of tax exemption for churches is clear: the foundation has been laid for taxing church property and perhaps even church income.

As Justice Douglas pointed out in *Walz v. Tax Commission*, the long and unbroken history of tax exemption for religious organizations should not be taken lightly. Nor should the reason for not taxing churches be overlooked.

First, tax exemption for churches has helped a pluralistic society in which a broad spectrum of religious perspectives—including irreligion—can flourish. Such pluralism safeguards against extremism and should be maintained.

Neither Sponsorship nor Hostility

The legislative purpose of a property tax exemption is neither the advancement nor the inhibition of religion; it is neither sponsorship nor hostility. New York, in common with the other States, has determined that certain entities that exist in a harmonious relationship to the community at large, and that foster its "moral or mental improvement," should not be inhibited in their activities by property taxation or the hazard of loss of those properties for nonpayment of taxes. It has not singled out one particular church or religious group or even churches as such; rather, it has granted exemption to all houses of religious worship.

Warren E. Burger, *Walz v. Tax Commission of the City of New York*, 1970.

Second, taxing church property and income would destroy the free exercise of religion that the Bill of Rights seeks to protect. The old principle that the power to tax is the power to destroy is still valid. In regard to taxing door-to-door religious solicitation, the Court held in *Murdock v. Pennsylvania* in 1943:

> The power to tax the exercise of a privilege is the power to control or suppress its enjoyment. . . . Those who can tax the exercise of this religious practice can make its exercise so costly as to deprive it of the resources necessary for its maintenance.

The power to tax religious institutions must be construed as the power to limit the free exercise of religion. Levying property taxes upon churches would have the effect of closing the doors of thousands of small congregations that operate on a shoestring. Many downtown churches would be forced out by the property taxes on their valuable land, and their buildings would be replaced by high-rise office complexes.

A third reason for not taxing church property is the excessive government entanglement that such taxation would bring. What agency would be responsible for assessing the value of the property, and how would the value be calculated? To what extent will the government require inspection of church property and, in the process, its records? These are but a few areas of church-state entanglement that would come with church property taxes. Of course, with government intervention comes government regulation, which could extend into many aspects of church life. Such entanglement must be viewed as unconstitutional.

As the budget deficits of the federal, state and local governments increase, the possibility of taxing church property also rises—despite the long history of tax exemption. To help avert such an occurrence, religious groups must become alert to court actions on church-state issues, and they must become more vocal in asserting the constitutionality of church property tax exemption.

"Exempting the churches from the ordinary burdens imposed upon all citizens . . . [is] a violation of the 'establishment clause.'"

Taxing Church Property Would Restore Civil Liberties

American Atheist

American Atheist magazine is published monthly by American Atheists, a nonprofit organization dedicated to the complete and absolute separation of church and state. The organization has led many campaigns to abolish tax exemptions for churches. In the following viewpoint, the editors contend that if the government exempts churches from taxation, it is violating the First Amendment.

As you read, consider the following questions:

1. Why did Jon G. Murray, president of American Atheists, recommend that the Texas legislature tax churches?
2. How does tax exemption violate the Constitution, according to the authors?
3. According to *American Atheist,* tax exemption advances religion. Do you agree or disagree?

American Atheist, "Why Tax Church Property," May 1987. Reprinted with permission from the *American Atheist.*

Early in the fall of 1986, it became obvious that Texas was in extreme financial difficulties and its governor, Mark White, faced the Texas legislature in special session over the crisis of emergency funding. American Atheists contacted every state legislator, the governor, the secretary of state, and the media suggesting a remedy for the state deficit: putting a squeeze on the churches and religious institutions in Texas. Four sources of revenue could be found for the state in such an exercise including:

1. the discontinuance of tax exemptions on the enormous land holdings of churches and religious organizations in Texas, cited in the October 1986 issue of *Texas Business* as well in excess of $45 billion;
2. a special tax on income from bingo and lottery games run primarily by the Roman Catholic church in Texas;
3. the discontinuance of tax funding for religious institutions of all kinds, but particularly for religious schools;
4. a special tax on income from stock/bond portfolio holdings of churches and religious organizations.

Jon G. Murray, president of American Atheists, offered to address the Texas legislature and to apprise both houses of the fallacies of the positions which are constantly advanced in support of complete exemption from taxes to churches and religious institutions. He summarized these briefly as follows.

Violating the Constitution

So long as the tax exemption deals equally with all religions, without discrimination, the constitution is not violated.

We must recognize that the exemption is a subsidy from the state in direct proportion to the amount of taxable property which the religious organization owns. The exemptions are not, therefore, equally applicable to all religions, or all sects of the Judeo-Christian religion. Exemptions fall with largess upon the largest landholders. The land-rich denominations have a clear advantage over those which do not own large tracts of land. Members of the poorer congregations are put in the position of contributing to the support of the land-rich denominations by an increased rate of taxation upon their individual property. . . .

The Constitution guarantees there will be no laws "prohibiting the free exercise of religion." Ending religious exemptions would hamper the free exercise of religion by church members.

The Free Exercise clause of the First Amendment protects the rights to prayer, Mass, sermons, sacraments, and all practices of religious beliefs. Ad valorem tax is a nondiscriminatory fee placed alike on all who desire to hold land. It is not aimed at either promotion or restriction of religious belief. The First Amendment also protects freedom of speech but does not relieve owners of printing houses from taxes upon their land. The First Amendment does not require a subsidy be given in the form of fiscal exemptions from taxes for "free exercise." Freedom from taxation is not a prerequisite attached to the privilege.

The state must protect the rights of the religious people.

The term *religious people* is not synonymous with the term *churchgoer* in our nation. The state must also protect those who do not attend churches out of their own choice. Going to or staying away from church, or membership in a church, is a matter of private decision. The state cannot burden the nonchurchgoer with taxes in order to give relief to persons who desire to be "churched." Nonchurchgoers are taxpayers with personal and proprietary interest in the matter of reduced taxation. If they desire to contribute to the churches, they could do this simply by attending churches or giving donations to them. The discrimination here is against nonchurch members. Government compulsion is used to extract higher property taxes. This is an indirect means of obtaining money from the general taxpayer which he would not, of his volition, otherwise give. . . .

Taxes Are Not Entanglement

One has only to look at the situation of hard and electronic media—newspapers and magazines, radio and television. "Freedom of speech" is protected by the First Amendment to the Constitution of the United States also. But this does not give the media the right to demand exemption from all taxation, or to demand subsidization by government from tax funds. Generally speaking, taxes run with the land. The religious organizations simply should be put on notice that there will be no laws passed making them immune from such tax. If they desire land, the land and the taxes are inseparable, and they should and must pay whatever taxes are levied. There is no "entanglement" here of any kind. Religious organizations have telephone service, and they are billed for it and pay the revenue expected. There is no "entanglement" with the telephone company. For the U.S. Supreme Court to pretend to an entanglement which does not exist is deception.

American Atheist, May 1987.

The repercussions of abolishing religious exemptions would redound against the court which so decided, to a greater extent than the decision to remove Bible and prayer from the public schools.

Our courts are not established to curry favor with majorities. The National Council of Churches reports that the influence of churches might be less than is assumed. As reported by that organization, for some years, the percentages of persons feeling that religion is losing its influence has constantly increased.

In any event, the U.S. Supreme Court has weathered other

storms: desegregation; one-man, one-vote; etc.

Churches are above the law: this is religion.

In the United States we begin with the premise of equal rights to all men and women. The claim of religion is that of a superior right because of certain ideas that religious people hold. They ask to be free of the ordinary burdens of society at the expense of those who support the society generally.

There are four hundred-plus brands of religion in the United States, all claiming to be the "one true faith." These include godless, prayerless, and heavenless groups of all kinds including Buddhists, Taoists, Ethical Culturists, Humanists, and New Age. Religion is merely set apart from government in our nation, not above it. Each religion has full liberty to spread its doctrines at its own cost. Whether one or any particular group or all religions thrive or decline is none of the business of the state. All the state can do is to give a free field to all, and then let them succeed or fail in proportion to their own merits and their ability to convince men and women of their truth and of the merits of their claim to monetary support at the hands of the individuals thus convinced. No amount of sophistry can disguise the fact that a church is primarily a doctrinal organization and among the Judeo-Christian sects there is no clear and compelling support to the claims of any to be above the law.

American Atheists would recall to you the words of Benjamin Franklin: "When a religion is good, I conceive it will support itself; and when it does not support itself, and God does not take care to support it so that its professors are obliged to call for help of the civil power, it's a sign, I apprehend, of its being a bad one.". . .

Respecting Separation of Church and State

The tax exemption is only an indirect subsidy and is not a breach of the wall of separation of state and church.

There is no secular legislative purpose stated in any of the constitutions or statutes of any of the states of the United States in respect to tax exemption of churches or religious organizations. The primary effect of all of these laws, and particularly that of Texas, is to advance religion. The exemption is a classification solely in terms of religion. The classifications exempt only those activities which are religious, exempts only those properties with a religious alliance or use, always in sectarian fashion. The government cannot thus go into the business of indirectly aiding religion which the government is forbidden directly by the Establishment Clause of the First Amendment to the Constitution of the United States.

In the case of *Walz* v. *Tax Commission of City of New York*, (1970), the fact situation was different. The plaintiff was a religious man and hence, with religion deemed by him to be good, really had no argument for not supporting the idea. In the case filed in Texas: (1) All of the plaintiffs are Atheists and/or Atheist organizations. (2) They see religion as inimical to the interests of humankind. (3) They challenge that the place of religious worship, the church itself, and all of its associated activities are being subsidized by the state in the form of a tax exemption. (4) The harm to them is that it increases the tax that they must pay since land owned by religious organizations is excluded from the tax base. (5) The constitution of the state of Texas provides specific relief to the churches, but at the same time (6) guarantees that no man may be forced against his profession to support those churches. The consequence of the exemption laws is that Atheists in Texas are required to support religious institutions and churches directly through increased taxes on their land.

Exemption Is Unfair

All of the churches use the public services and public agencies which make their churches usable; roads, traffic control, fire and police protection, water treatment and sewers, street lighting, public administration, and so forth.

But religious tax exemption lets these people withhold from real estate, real property, sales, and income taxes that share which is exempt. Of course, our public treasuries will continue to shrink every year as churchists help to increase the need for public expenditures. The shrink is exactly consonant with the amount which gives churches relief from their duties to meet church demands.

S.J. Wilson, *The Humanist*, January/February 1984.

Additionally, (7) American Atheists are in agreement (except for the theist palaver) with James Madison who wrote in his *Memorial and Remonstrance Against Religious Assessments:*

> Whilst we assert for ourselves a freedom to embrace, to profess and to observe the Religion which we believe to be of divine origin, we cannot deny an equal freedom to those whose minds have not yet yielded to the evidence which has convinced us. If this freedom be abused, it is an offense against God, not against man: to God, therefore, not to men, must an account be rendered. As the Bill [Assessment Bill to levy a tax for the support of Christian churches in Virginia, in 1784-5] violates equality by subjecting some to peculiar burdens; so it violates the same principle, by granting to others peculiar exemptions.

In the present situation, Atheists and theists are treated differently only because of the articles of faith of the theists.

American Atheists is not seeking to "Tax the Church." Its officers and members simply feel that if ad valorem tax for the support of our public school system runs with the land, the churches should not be given exemption from it. Rather, the churches should be circumspect about grabbing up as much land as they can and should be made fully aware that taxes will continue to run with that land. Religious groups cannot be free from all financial burdens of government.

The First Amendment to the Constitution (in the Bill of Rights), states, "Congress shall make no law respecting an establishment of religion, or preventing the free exercise thereof. . . ."

"Congress" has been translated by the U.S. Supreme Court to mean any part of government, state as well as federal, city as well as county since the Fourteenth Amendment made the First Amendment applicable to all of the states. When one of these government entities "makes a law" specifically exempting the churches from the ordinary burdens imposed upon all citizens, American Atheists holds that to be a violation of the "establishment clause."

Recognizing Statements That Are Provable

From various sources of information we are constantly confronted with statements and generalizations about social and moral problems. In order to think clearly about these problems, it is useful if one can make a basic distinction between statements for which evidence can be found and other statements which cannot be verified or proved because evidence is not available, or the issue is so controversial that it cannot be definitely proved.

Readers should be aware that magazines, newspapers and other sources often contain statements of a controversial nature. The following activity is designed to allow experimentation with statements that are provable and those that are not.

The following statements are taken from the viewpoints in this chapter. Consider each statement carefully. *Mark P for any statement you believe is provable. Mark U for any statement you feel is unprovable because of the lack of evidence. Mark C for any statements you think are too controversial to be proved to everyone's satisfaction.*

If you are doing this activity as a member of a class or group, compare your answers with those of other class or group members. Be able to defend your answers. You may discover that others will come to different conclusions than you. Listening to the reasons others present for their answers may give you valuable insights in recognizing statements that are provable.

> P = *provable*
> U = *unprovable*
> C = *too controversial*

1. Government intrusion into religious practices constitutes a clear and present danger to our constitutional rights.

2. James Madison contended that support of religion should be voluntary.

3. The framers of the Constitution all came from religious families.

4. The Federal Equal Access bill did not become a law.

5. Opposition to governmental support of religion is usually confused with opposition to religion itself.

6. Only a clear separation of church and state can adequately protect each from domination by the other.

7. A state university can legally deny student religious groups use of its facilities for the purpose of worship.

8. Taxing church property is unconstitutional.

9. The federal deficit would be much smaller if churches had to pay taxes.

10. Congress has never specifically exempted religious bodies from real estate taxes.

11. The American Atheists group favors taxation of churches.

12. Atheist groups are envious of religious groups' tax-exempt status.

13. Making public school students study religion violates their civil rights.

14. There is nothing in any Supreme Court ruling prohibiting a student from praying while in school.

15. Public school students are less disciplined because religious instruction is no longer allowed in their schools.

16. Human beings need to have religion as part of their right to the pursuit of happiness.

17. The US Constitution's provision for the separation of church and state is applicable only on the federal level, not the state level.

18. Separation of church and state is currently an important issue only because a growing number of Americans are rejecting religious authority.

19. Religion is an inherent part of human experience and therefore cannot be separated from human government.

Periodical Bibliography

The following articles have been selected to supplement the diverse views presented in this chapter.

America	"Religious Education and Public Schools," October 25, 1986.
Christianity Today	"Debate: Should the US Supreme Court Play an Activist Role?" March 21, 1986.
Charles Colson	"Friends of Religious Liberty: Why the Embarrassing Silence?" *Christianity Today*, April 18, 1986.
Jerry H. Combee	"Evangelicals and the First Amendment," *National Review*, October 24, 1986.
Robert L. Cord	"Founding Intentions: Correcting the Record," *National Review*, April 11, 1986.
Donald W. Foster	"God and the IRS," *The Humanist*, January/February 1984.
Os Guinness	"Where Celebration Is Not Enough," *Vital Speeches of the Day*, December 15, 1986.
Robert P. Hay	"The Faith of the Founding Fathers," *USA Today*, May 1986.
Peter Huidekoper Jr.	"God and Man in the Classroom," *Newsweek*, April 2, 1984.
Kenneth S. Kantzer	"Should Government Subsidize the Church?" *Christianity Today*, April 8, 1983.
Charles W. Kegley	"Church-State Relations Are Heating Up," *USA Today*, January 1986.
Robert L. Maddox	"Church and State: The Ramparts Besieged," *The Christian Century*, February 25, 1987.
Terry Muck	"The Wall that Never Was," *Christianity Today*, July 10, 1987.
Richard John Neuhaus	"Religious Liberty," *Vital Speeches of the Day*, July 15, 1986.
Donald W. Schriver Jr.	"A Religious Argument Against School Prayer," *USA Today*, May 1984.
Rosemary Zagarri	"Founding Intentions: Jefferson and Madison on School Prayer," *The New Republic*, September 9, 1985.

How Free Should Speech Be?

CIVIL LIBERTIES
OPPOSING VIEWPOINTS

Chapter Preface

Many people consider the First Amendment to be the cornerstone of America's freedom. The freedom to say what one wishes no matter what political faction is in power, to worship as one believes whether or not one's religious group is in the mainstream, to publish what one wants regardless of whether it concurs with popular opinion, and to come together to support or protest public policy without fear of reprisal are all rights belonging to US citizens. These rights are what many people believe make America the free, democratic, and independent nation it is.

This chapter focuses specifically on freedom of speech, one right protected by the First Amendment. While the Amendment may appear to be unambiguous, interpretation as to what it actually protects inspires heated debate. There are those who believe that the First Amendment protects every kind of speech, including the most offensive or threatening. Others believe that there are some kinds of speech—such as pornography, racist demagoguery, inflammatory political speech, and speech that promotes violence—that are so offensive they should not be tolerated.

The authors of the following viewpoints focus on the issue of whether all speech must be allowed in a country such as the US or whether some speech cannot—indeed, should not—be protected.

> *"'The danger that citizens will think wrongly is . . . less dangerous than atrophy from not thinking at all.'"*

Free Speech Must Be Absolute

Richard Moon

Richard Moon, a member of the Bar of Ontario, writes in the following viewpoint that one of the most important functions served by freedom of speech is the development of rational thought, moral judgment, emotional attachment, and the sense of community. It is vital, he states, not to inhibit these qualities by suppressing free speech.

As you read, consider the following questions:

1. What does Moon say is the most important value of freedom of expression?
2. Moon states that "the good of the individual is bound up with the community." How, then, does freedom of expression aid the nation?
3. Why does Moon believe that free speech must not be limited?

Richard Moon, "The Scope of Freedom of Expression," *Osgoode Hall Law Journal*, Summer 1985. Reprinted with permission.

Traditionally, two arguments have been made in support of freedom of expression. The first is that the freedom is an important prerequisite to democracy. Protection must be given to any expression which is necessary to the operation of a representative form of government. The second argument is that the freedom must be protected if we are to respect the "autonomy" of the individual. An "autonomous" person is one who is free to express himself or herself to others and to receive the communications of others without interference by the state.

Both these theories offer little guidance as to the proper scope of the freedom because neither gives a complete explanation of the freedom. What sort of expression is necessary to the operation of democratic government? If "democracy" means representative government, then only a very narrow category of human expression will fall within the freedom's scope. Representative government can exist in a community where dance, painting and music are subject to censorship. Indeed, representative government can exist where most discussion is proscribed. So long as citizens are able to vote and to communicate with their elected representatives, the government will be representative.

But the term "democracy" sometimes refers to something more than a form of government. It sometimes refers to a social context in which an individual is able to participate in various social goods and to develop as a free and thinking person. If this is what "democracy" means, then the scope of the freedom will be much broader. . . .

Autonomy

The term "autonomy" is also defined in different ways. Ordinarily those who see "autonomy" as the justification for the freedom use the term to mean the absence of external barriers to an individual's actions—drawing on the liberal idea that the state ought not to favour one individual's conception of the good over another's. If "autonomy" in this sense is the basis of freedom of expression then the freedom's scope will be very broad indeed—covering every action of the individual. If any form of external restraint is *prima facie* wrong, then no particular category of human action is set apart for special protection. All action must be protected. This is a wide claim for a constitutional right—even one subject to reasonable limits. . . .

But often the term "autonomy" refers to a capacity in individuals to make choices and to conduct their lives in a way that is true to their purposes. If freedom of expression is based on "autonomy" in this sense then its scope will be something less than all human actions. Its scope will extend only to those forms of expression which are of particular significance to the development and exercise of the individual's capacity for intelligent and morally sensitive thought. . . .

When we look closely at both "democratic" and "autonomy"-based theories, we can see that they point to another explanation of the freedom. They suggest that the justification for freedom of expression lies not in the value of "democratic" (meaning representative) government or individual "autonomy" (meaning liberty) but in the value of social interaction. Through communication with one another we experience certain forms of good and we develop fully as human beings.

If we see individual development not as the surfacing of a personality which is already set, but as the growth of certain human capacities, then the significance of the freedom becomes clearer. Through communication we develop as human beings in the capacities we value such as rational thought, moral judgment and emotional attachment. . . . If we hold that certain capacities are valuable, it follows that we should not impair their exercise. It also follows that we should try to create an environment in which human capacities are encouraged to develop. Freedom of expression is an important part of such an environment.

Protecting Ideas We Hate

It's easy to embrace freedom of speech for ideas we accept. The essence of freedom of speech and the press is that we must protect the ideas we hate.

Harriet Pilpel, in *The Meese Commission Exposed*, The National Coalition Against Censorship, 1986.

The importance of freedom of expression to individual development explains why we should not prevent individuals from expressing their views or prevent them from hearing the views of others, even when we may properly criticize those views and pass laws which prevent them from being put into effect. Allowing individuals to hear and assess the views of others is no guarantee that they will always make wise decisions, but this freedom is essential if they are to develop as thinking beings capable of making judgments. As Mr. Justice Jackson of the American Supreme Court said, "[t]he danger that citizens will think wrongly is serious but less dangerous than atrophy from not thinking at all."

Truth

John Stuart Mill supported freedom of expression on the utilitarian ground that the truth is most likely to emerge in a society that permits the unrestricted exchange of ideas. But in Mill's writing there are frequent suggestions that the freedom may also be justified because consideration of different points of view will cultivate intellect and judgment. This shift in Mill's argument from truth to capacity to recognize truth protects Mill from the standard attacks made against the claim that the freedom is justified because truth is most likely to emerge from its exercise. For there are times when the truth will not emerge from the marketplace of ideas (the general community and particular individuals will make mistakes) and sometimes, with little danger of error, the state can censor certain ideas and protect the individual from coming to hold false beliefs. If truth and only truth is what we value, then censorship is entirely sensible. By censoring false ideas, the state can limit their spread. But if we value the capacity to make judgments about truth then censorship of any idea, true or false, makes no sense.

As well it is essential to the development of individuals that they be allowed to express their views to others. In articulating their ideas, individuals give shape to that which is initially inchoate and confused. In expressing themselves to others they become "individuals" with a particular personality and point of view. As Charles Taylor has observed:

> [S]peech [is] the activity by which we gain a kind of explicit self-aware consciousness of things which as such is always related to an unreflective experience which precedes it and which it illuminates and hence transforms.

But communication is valuable in another way. By communicating we participate in certain forms of "human good": knowledge, friendship, self-government and other activities or ways of life that are valuable. Communication or social interaction is an end in itself. By communicating an individual forms relationships and associations with others—family, friends, coworkers, church congregation, countrymen. By entering into discussion with others an individual participates in the development of knowledge and in the direction of the community.

The value attached to freedom of expression, then, is based on a recognition that the good of the individual is bound up with the community. Expression is the way we interact with others and so participate in social goods such as friendship and self-government. And through expression individuals develop their human capacities. . . .

Free Speech and the Social Good

It is sometimes argued that freedom of expression must give way when the interests of unity and stability are threatened by the spread of anti-democratic or anti-social ideas. But the freedom of expression rests upon the belief that an individual must be free to communicate with others even though he sometimes will be in error or sometimes will dissent from views thought to be fundamental and even though those who receive his communication believe his mistaken or anti-social views. If an individual is to participate in the "social goods" and develop as a human being, he must have this freedom.

Killing Ideas

Every attempt to censor is an attempt to kill an idea. Sometimes the idea is trivial—kids should buy Gummi Bears, for example. Sometimes it seems trivial in one age and vital in another. . . .

Sometimes the censors speak for national security, sometimes for public morals. But always they speak for fear. Fear that their opponents' ideas will persuade. Fear that their own arguments, values, and beliefs will be found wanting. Fear that free people, left to their own devices, will fall into evil ways. Americans have come to accept such fears, to readily grant exceptions to the rule of free speech. And *that* is reason to be afraid.

Virginia I. Postrel, *Reason*, October 1987.

Is there a point at which the freedom must surrender to the pressing needs of social unity—of "community"? I do not believe there is such a point. "Community," in the sense of a "sharing of life or of action or of interests, an associating or coming together," is a "social good" which develops through the freedom of expression. By protecting voluntary social interaction, the freedom makes social co-operation and unity possible. Unity and social solidarity only exist, in any real sense, when individuals are free to make judgments and direct their lives. If communication were suppressed, the result would be a population which was inhibited in its ability to reflect upon important questions of value and a society which was closed and rigid rather than "free and democratic."

"The ends of the First Amendment . . . are not compatible with everything that it enters into the mind of man to utter."

Free Speech Must Be Limited

Francis Canavan

Francis Canavan, a Jesuit priest, is on the faculty of Fordham University in New York. In the following viewpoint, he argues that it is only common sense that expression must sometimes be limited. He states that not only are some forms of expression not worth protecting, but that unlimited freedom ultimately results in chaos, meaninglessness, and loss of true freedom.

As you read, consider the following questions:

1. Canavan describes three ways a scene in a hypothetical war movie might be filmed. Why does he believe the third version should not be protected by the First Amendment?
2. The author states that "even a false idea or . . . an evil idea" might be protected by the First Amendment, but that appeals "to mere passion" do not deserve protection. How does he explain this?
3. What danger does Canavan perceive if free speech is absolutely unlimited?

Francis Canavan, *Freedom of Expression: Purpose as Limit.* Durham, NC: Carolina Academic Press, 1984. Reprinted with permission.

Freedom of speech, without distinctions among kinds of speech, is no more defensible than an unqualified freedom of action, and no more desirable. A free society, after all, is as much a society in which people are free to act as one in which they are free to talk. . . . Yet freedom to act does not include freedom to perform every action, or any action in all circumstances, nor does it imply that every action is of equal value in the eyes of the law and, consequently, equally subject to or immune from restraint. . . .

An Example

To take a hypothetical example, let us suppose that three directors film the same battle scene in three distinct films. The first director films the battle as an adventure and wishes to communicate the experience of danger faced and overcome, of victory achieved and glory won. His film may also be intended to serve as propaganda for a "hawkish" U.S. foreign policy. The second director films the battle in order to communicate an experience of the horrors of war and to induce a revulsion against it. His film may, in addition, be intended to serve as propaganda for a "dovish" U.S. foreign policy. But, whatever one may think of either director's point of view, his filming of the battle scene communicates an acceptable vicarious experience and is a legitimate exercise of freedom of the press.

In contrast, the third director films the battle as an exercise in sadism. What he communicates is a vicarious experience of the pleasure of inflicting pain, death and degradation on human beings. To picture soldiers beating their enemies to death with their rifle butts is shocking but, properly handled, it can be a realistic portrayal of war and can serve a legitimate artistic end. But at some point of gruesomeness, such a portrayal will pass beyond any legitimate end. If the camera dwells long and lovingly on a man's face being beaten into a bloody and shapeless mass until it is no longer recognizably human, the suspicion and finally the certainty grows that what is being appealed to is nothing more than a sick appetite for violence. It is submitted that, with all due presumptions in favor of artistic freedom, reason can sometimes recognize such an appeal so clearly and unmistakably as to judge it unworthy of constitutional protection. For, if freedom of expression is not an absolute end in itself, judgment must be passed on that which is expressed, and not everything that can be expressed serves the ends of the First Amendment.

It is too narrow an interpretation of freedom of speech and press to confine its protection to appeals to the mind through reasoned discourse. Appeals to the imagination and emotions through literature and the arts also deserve protection. But there is a sense in which every kind of utterance ought to be subject to reason

103

under the First Amendment. To decide the constitutionality of limiting or suppressing an utterance requires passing rational judgment on the ends which the utterance serves and rational evaluation of those ends in the light of the purposes of the First Amendment. . . .

Free Speech and Reason

Reason can approve of much that it cannot prove. Religious belief depends on faith rather than on rational demonstration, and the same can be said of political and other kinds of belief. But belief can be advocated and defended rationally. Even a false idea or, for that matter, an evil idea can serve the cause of truth if an effort is made to present the grounds for it (however specious) in the manner appropriate to rational argument and it is subjected to rational criticism. Literature and the arts, as we have said, appeal to the imagination and the emotions as much or more than to naked reason, yet they, too, are subject to rational judgment and should serve ends of which reason can approve. All of these, as well as the kind of expression that seeks to engender complete rational conviction through demonstrative argument, deserve constitutional protection. But the appeal to mere passion, uncontrolled by reason and directed to irrational or anti-rational purposes, does not deserve protection because it does not serve what Justice Jackson called "the great end for which the First Amendment stands."

Restraint Enhances Freedom

The justices of the Supreme Court have understood what the ancients understood: some sense of restraint is absolutely essential to maintaining a free, democratic society over the long term. In that sense, the concept of *limits* is the friend, not the enemy, of individual liberty. Let us not forget that idea, lest "our children wake to discover, as Saint Augustine lamented in his *Confessions,* 'Too late I loved you, O Beauty ever ancient and ever new. Too late I loved you! And behold, you were within me, and I out of myself, and there I searched for you.'"

Bruce C. Hafen, speech to Religious Alliance Against Pornography, November 13, 1986.

The objection usually alleged against allowing the law any power over speech or publication that appeals to sexual lust is that "obscenity" is beyond the ability of law adequately to define. Justice Stewart, for example, was laughed at for saying that, while he could not define hardcore pornography, "I know it when I see it." But consider the following lines from *Time* for April 6, 1970. After the fall of Prince Sihanouk from power in Cambodia, the magazine reported, the "local press mocked him savagely and his half-Italian wife Princess Monique even more. Some newspapers ran composite photos of her head on anonymous nude bodies in obscene poses." The editors of *Time* evidently assumed that their readers would have no difficulty in understanding what those words meant, and the people in Cambodia who made up and published the composite photographs took it for granted that their readers would know an obscene pose when they saw one. To bring the matter closer to home, if one's sister, wife or daughter posed in the nude for a photographer, would it make any difference what poses she was asked to assume? Or would one feel obliged to maintain that a truly liberal and objective mind could recognize no meaningful differences among poses? Anyone who would honestly have to admit that he could recognize differences and find them significant should be willing to admit that a jury could do so, too. It was, in fact, to juries, properly instructed in the legal norms and subject to review by appellate courts, that the Supreme Court assigned the function of recognizing obscenity for what it is.

The Court also found a public interest important enough to justify state regulation or suppression of obscene material. "The sum of experience, including that of the past two decades," it said in June, 1973, "affords an ample basis for legislatures to conclude that a sensitive, key relationship of human existence, central to family life, community welfare, and the development of human personality, can be debased and distorted by crass commercial exploitation of sex." In an implicit rejection of *The Report of the [Presidential] Commission on Obscenity and Pornography*, the Court added: "Nothing in the Constitution prohibits a State from reaching such a conclusion and acting on it legislatively simply because there is no conclusive evidence or empirical data." After all, it pointed out, legislatures had acted in many fields on indemonstrable assumptions, yet the Court had upheld their legislation. In saying this, far from abandoning reason, the Court realistically recognized the way in which reason acts and must act in the regulation of human affairs.

Rational vs. Irrational

Ultimately, then, the line drawn by the First Amendment is not simply between speech and conduct but between irrational and more or less rational speech. The presumption in every case favors freedom of utterance. But the presumption must sometimes yield to the claims of competing public interests. In such cases, the Court must take into account, not only the weight and value of the public interest alleged, but also the quality and comparative value of the kind of speech involved. This value will depend on the rationally discernible relationship of the speech in question to one or more of the ends of the First Amendment. In this sense, the unifying principle of the hierarchy of kinds of speech, for purposes of constitutional adjudication, is rationality.

In addition to the two basic scales—kinds of speech and levels of public interest—that are weighed against each other in constitutional adjudication, we may postulate another scale, that of the manners or modes of expression. Independently of the content of an utterance, the way in which it is uttered may make it more or less deserving of constitutional protection. Justice Stewart once wrote that "the Constitution protects coarse expression as well as refined, and vulgarity no less than elegance." It is true that the Constitution was not written for a nation made up exclusively of ladies and gentlemen, and that it protects a large range of expressions that are neither refined nor elegant. It does not follow that there are and ought to be no limits on the kind of language one is permitted to use in public, on the visual imagery that one may set before the public's eye, or on the kind and volume of noise which one may inflict on the public's ears. The more offensive an utterance becomes in its manner of expression (as distinct from its content), the more easily it may be subordinated to public propriety and comfort, and the more nearly it approaches the point where it loses its claim to constitutional protection. . . .

Legal Distinctions Are Essential

Law, as we have acknowledged, is a blunt instrument and not a surgeon's scalpel. But despite its necessary rigidity and bluntness, law can and must make distinctions and recognize degrees of difference in applying its general rules to the decision of particular cases. The distinctions will be more easily and more accurately made in regard to freedom of speech and press if we get back to asking, more insistently than we have in recent years, what are we trying to protect and why. Not everything that can be labelled "speech," or "expression," or "utterance" is worth protecting. Much of it must be granted immunity for the sake of preserving the freedom of speech and press that serves the ends of the First Amendment. But not all of it need be or should be rendered immune from legal regulation for the general good. The ends of the First Amendment, broad though they are, are not compatible with everything that it enters into the mind of man to utter, in any way in which he chooses to utter it. The quest for rationality in interpreting the amendment's guarantees of freedom of speech and press forces us to ask, in the end, what the freedom is for.

Free Speech and True Freedom

Divorced from their original purpose, Walter Lippmann once wrote, "freedom to think and speak are not self-evident necessities. It is only from the hope and the intention of discovering truth that freedom acquires such high public significance." But, he warned, when the chaff of silliness, baseness, and deception is so voluminous that it submerges the kernels of truth, freedom of speech may produce such frivolity, or such mischief, that it cannot be preserved against the demand for a restoration of order or of decency. If there is a dividing line between liberty and license, it is where freedom of speech is no longer respected as a procedure of the truth and becomes the unrestricted right to exploit the ignorance, and to incite the passions, of the people. Then freedom is such a hullabaloo of sophistry, propaganda, special pleading, lobbying and salesmanship that it is difficult to remember why freedom of speech is worth the pain and trouble of defending it.

Lippmann's words state the contemporary problem well. It is not to push back ever farther the outer limits of freedom of speech and press, but to remember ever more clearly why the freedom was worth defending in the first place. For when the purpose of freedom is forgotten, freedom cannot long survive.

"In a given situation, failure to repress speech because of its content can . . . be dangerous."

Some Views May Be Suppressed

Randall Kennedy

When the "speech" of two parties is in direct conflict, do both parties have equal rights even if one interferes with the other? In the following viewpoint, Randall Kennedy, an assistant professor at Harvard Law School and a member of the Massachusetts Civil Liberties Union, argues that certain kinds of speech are so inhumane that not to suppress them is dangerous to society. In this viewpoint he is responding to columnist Nat Hentoff's criticism of views he articulated when a pro-apartheid speaker was invited to speak on Harvard's campus.

As you read, consider the following questions:

1. Kennedy points out several forms of "speech" that are not protected by the First Amendment. List them.
2. Kennedy states that his critics, specifically Hentoff, are themselves repressive in insisting on inflexible rules of free expression. What does Kennedy mean?
3. Why does the author believe that, despite the ideal of free speech, protestors who manage to suppress abhorent speech are doing the right thing?
4. Does Kennedy believe that anybody who feels like it should be free to disrupt a speech?

Randall Kennedy, "This Professor Says Free Speech Is Fine—Up to a Point (Cont'd)," *The Washington Post*, June 27, 1987. © The Washington Post.

South Africa is a pigmentocracy in which a white minority rules over a black majority by dint of sheer terror. Officials practice torture in South African jails, and scores of political prisoners have been killed while in police custody. Although blacks constitute about 70 percent of the population, they have no say in the government under which they suffer.

It is right and just for Americans to demonstrate their opposition to apartheid. But the justice of their cause does not exempt them from dilemmas involving the morality of political action. For instance, controversy has surrounded cases of collegiate anti-apartheid activists who disrupt pro-apartheid speeches by officials of the South African regime.

Such activists are certain to be condemned by reactionary bigots who embrace the idea of freedom of expression only when it can be used to whip leftish dissidents into line. But they will also likely be criticized by persons or organizations whose views on racial justice and civil liberties are entitled to respect; I think here particularly of the American Civil Liberties Union. All will resort to a set of precepts that exalt equal, neutral, symmetrical tolerance.

Many civil libertarians assert that all speakers invited to a campus must be allowed a hearing. Nat Hentoff implicitly adopts this position in a column in which he criticizes my contention that, in some circumstances, disruption of speech because of its content may be justified. The editors' headline on the column reads, "This Professor Says Free Speech is Fine—Up to a Point," as if it is somehow deviant to believe that freedom of speech should have limits.

Freedom Must Have Some Bounds

But even the ACLU recognizes that in any decent society freedom of speech must have some bounds. For without bounds, this freedom—like any freedom—can turn into an oppressive force. As President Derek Bok of Harvard University has observed, with respect to freedom of expression on campus, "free speech, though extremely important, must be fitted together with other rights and legitimate interests."

Civil libertarian absolutists such as Nat Hentoff fail to grapple with the complexities posed by clashing interests and instead seek security in automatic responses to abstract rules that disregard context. That is one reason why the contours of freedom of expression are undergoing spirited reappraisal from a wide array of perspectives. Conservatives such as George Will, feminists such as Catharine MacKinnon and liberals such as Owen Fiss have become understandably dissatisfied with explanations that neither explain the actual regulation of speech in society nor generate an inspiring vision of better arrangements.

It won't do to say categorically that suppression based on the content of speech is always wrong; what about proscriptions against perjury, threats, obscenity, libel, "fighting words," misleading advertising, invasion of privacy, advertisements for employment that exclude women or minorities, advocacy directed to inciting imminent unlawful action? It won't do to say simply that actions silencing speech can be dangerous; in a given situation, failure to repress speech because of its content can also be dangerous. It won't do to say unequivocally that tolerance is a virtue; tolerance may merely signal fear, or callousness, or the smug confidence of the strong.

Appalled by my argument that suppression of inhumane expressive conduct is sometimes justified, Hentoff asks: "Would [Kennedy] approve his students' taking over his class if they found him 'inhumane'?" If in fact I did act in a sufficiently offensive manner, a student takeover of my class might be justified, although my position as a professor should give me extraordinary leeway. If I repeatedly stated in my course on contracts that Jews or blacks or Asian Americans are genetically incapable of trustworthy behavior, there would indeed come a point at which the students in the class could legitimately disrupt it. Ironically, while Hentoff accuses me of being suppressive, it is he who would apparently subject students, and society at large, to the tyranny of certain absolutely inflexible rules.

More Listener-Controlled Power

None of our freedoms are guaranteed, none are secure. And if democratic struggle has taught us anything, it is that our rights are *not* things which must be "preserved." Rather, they must be vigorously used and expanded. . . . Freedom of speech needs more militant application and less abstract admiration. . . .

We must push for . . . more listener-controlled access [to power]. In every field of endeavor we must learn to see the dimensions of a struggle that advances the interests of the many and opposes the interests of the exploitative and outrageously privileged few.

Michael Parenti, *The Witness*, September 1987.

Because freedom of expression is such a rightly cherished aspect of academic life and democratic government, university authorities should view disruption of a speaker as presumptively illegitimate. But protesters seeking to justify disruption should be allowed to meet that burden of proof by drawing attention to relevant considerations including the harms that would have likely ensued from the speech, the degree to which the speaker has access to other forums of communication, and the manner in which the dissidents accomplished their goal. Freedom resides not only with the speaker but with protesters, the immediate audience, the university community, and those beyond—including the blacks of South Africa.

Perhaps university authorities will not want to invest scarce resources in exhaustive case-by-case adjudication. In that event, they should make clear their rationale for disciplining disruption without pretending, as is often done, that suppressing speech is necessarily wrong.

Another concern is that even holding out the possibility of ex-oneration will accentuate the risk of additional disruptions. But under my terms protesters would have to shoulder a heavy burden of persuasion to escape censure.

Legitimate Disruption

Anti-apartheid activists justify their disruption on the ground that they have a legitimate interest in preventing South Africa from advancing its ideological war against racial justice. Appalled by the way the regime has stifled dissent at home, they contend that it would be unfair to allow the regime's officials to exploit the collegiate forum to praise a system that buries the hopes of nonwhite South Africans. Seared by the brutality of the South African state of emergency, they maintain that their actions constitute legitimate resistance to injustice and proper aid in the struggle for a more humane world.

Even if they are wrong on some levels, disruptive anti-apartheid activists are right in their empathetic response to those suffering under the horrors of the South African regime. And perhaps they are not wrong at all but correctly following wise institutions that history will vindicate.

"If we are not free to speak heresy and utter awful thoughts, we are not free at all."

All Views
Must Be Heard

Alan Dershowitz & Kurt Luedtke

Alan Dershowitz teaches at Harvard Law School and writes a syndicated newspaper column. Karl Leudtke, formerly an editor at the *Detroit Free Press*, is a screenwriter. Both writers strongly believe that democracy thrives only when every person is free to speak his or her mind, no matter how obnoxious or offensive the thought. In the following viewpoint, Dershowitz (Part I) and Luedtke (Part II) respond to the wave of demonstrations on US campuses that have prevented speakers from being heard.

As you read, consider the following questions:

1. Why does Dershowitz believe that even the most offensive speakers must be allowed to speak?
2. Does Dershowitz believe that those who object to a speaker's views must sit passively by and do nothing to express their disapproval?
3. Luedtke states that those who will not listen to another's view, no matter how offensive, are no longer citizens but are "part of the mob." What does he mean? Do you agree with him?

Alan Dershowitz, "Let Even the Most Obnoxious and Offensive Ideas Be Heard," *Los Angeles Times*, May 19, 1987. Reprinted by permission of United Feature Syndicate, Inc. Kurt Luedtke, "What Good Is Free Speech If No One Listens?" *Los Angeles Times*, January 7, 1987. Reprinted with permission.

I

Over the past decade, several Third World student organizations at Harvard University have provoked controversy by inviting officials of the Palestine Liberation Organization to speak. Not surprisingly, many Jewish students have objected to what they regard as a provocation. Some have picketed and leafleted, while others have hissed at some of the speakers' statements. No attempt has been made to prevent the PLO representatives from speaking, and there has been no physical violence. Nonetheless, some of the Third World students have castigated the Jewish students for not respecting principles of free speech.

Now the shoe appears to be on the other foot. During 1987, a right-wing political group at Harvard invited an official of South Africa's apartheid regime to speak. Several students tried to physically block the speaker—diplomat Duke Kent-Brown—and his speech had to be terminated prematurely.

The university rejected such intimidation as an inappropriate way to protest a speaker, and began disciplinary action against those involved.

Toleration Is Best

One of my colleagues, a brilliant and dedicated assistant professor of law who is a board member of the Massachusetts Civil Liberties Union, delivered a talk defending the disruption of such activities. . . . Here is what Prof. Randall Kennedy was reported as saying: "There comes a point where a speech is so far apart [from the community's values] it shouldn't be tolerated. . . . Whether or not you would be right in disrupting a speaker depends on what he was saying.". . .

I can understand why Kennedy, who is a black American fiercely opposed to apartheid, feels rage against an official representative of a racist regime that seeks to dehumanize the majority of its population because of its color. As an American Jew (who is also fiercely opposed to apartheid), I feel similar rage against representatives of terrorist groups, like the PLO, that target Jews for murder, or Nazi groups that call for genocide against my people.

Kennedy believes that "the people who invite (speakers like the South African official) are not authentically curious about what they have to say. I think it is a political action and not an educational endeavor." Many Jewish students similarly believed that the decision to invite PLO speakers was also more a political provocation than an educational experience. But political actions are often educational, even if not in the manner intended. Moreover, political actions are equally protected by principles of free speech as are educational ones.

Kennedy is profoundly wrong in suggesting that speech that

113

diverges widely from community values should not be tolerated. That is neither good education nor good politics.

There are many alternatives available to offended parties. They can boycott, picket, leaflet, debate, answer and even "boo" or "hiss" periodically to vocalize their disapproval—so long as the speaker is permitted to complete his message within reasonable bounds of civility and without threats of violence. The one option that is not available in a society committed to freedom of speech is for one group to prevent another group from listening to a speaker they wish to hear.

If a society—whether it be a government or a university—gives the power of censorship to any one group, it may not deny it to others with equally plausible claims. If students who are offended by South African apartheid can close that idea out of the marketplace, then by what principle could other students who are offended by abortion, atheism, homosexuality, feminism, sexism, socialism or capitalism be denied the power to close out those ideas? The result of giving one group the power to censor would be either inequality for other groups or pervasive censorship.

The Cost of Freedom

If we are wounded by an ugly idea, we must count it as part of the cost of freedom and, like American heroes in days gone by, bravely carry on.

Kurt Vonnegut, Jr., *Playboy*, January 1984.

It is best to tolerate even the most obnoxious and offensive ideas. We should be prepared to respond to the arguments of the racist who preaches apartheid, the terrorist who advocates murdering civilians, the fascist who justifies genocide and the communist who favors the suppression of basic liberties. We should trust our citizens—even our students—to reject these ideas. But only after they hear them.

II

I was for 15 years a journalist, a vocation in which you'd think you would learn a lot. I learned three things: The accused you've never met is more guilty than the one you've talked to. Truth and accuracy are not the same. Things are never, ever, as they appear to be.

Because I am less and less convinced of where the truth lies and more and more dubious of our ability to find it, I would like to point out a particular kind of responsibility—a personal responsibility—that I think is in danger of being unmet.

For better and often for worse, this is a pluralistic and democratic

114

society. It is relatively new and still experimental; it is probably only three or four generations ago that the country was effectively governed by an oligarchy that protected us from the tryanny of the majority. As we come closer and closer to true democracy, we are ever more susceptible to a certain kind of mob rule in which popularity substitutes for principle and consensus is mistaken for wisdom.

It is, I suppose, inevitable that we must pay a price for our exaltation of the common man; if, for instance, we measure democracy's viability by what the citizens choose to watch on television, I think we're entitled to question how in the world this electorate is entitled to be in charge of anything.

But we have no better idea. We can only hope that the rule of law and our willingness to abide by it will protect against the worst of which we are collectively capable.

Extraordinary Right to Personal Expression

It is the law in this country, as in no other, that the individual has an extraordinary right to personal expression. The First Amendment to the Constitution protects the right to speak and to publish; these rights and the degree to which they are safeguarded are the distinguishing characteristics of American society.

For that we have only the courts to thank. Americans seem to be almost completely uninterested in any point of view other than their individual own. We are absolutely up to our necks in groups and blocs and religious and economic interests certain beyond all reason that they are correct and actively interested in imposing their rules and values and self-selected morals on the rest of us. They prattle about democracy, and use it when it suits them without the slightest regard or respect for what it means and costs and requires. These people are—please believe me—dangerous.

The right to speak is meaningless if no one will listen, and the right to publish is not worth having if no one will read. It is simply not enough that we reject censorship and will not countenance suppression; we have an affirmative responsibility to hear the argument before we disagree with it.

I think that you think that you agree with me, that you are fair and open-minded and good citizens. But if we put it to the test—if I make up some speeches about gun control, abortion, gay rights, racial and ethnic characteristics, political terrorism and genocide—I believe that I can make you boo and jeer or at least walk out in protest.

We cannot operate that way. It's not difficult to listen to the philosophy you agree with or don't care about. It's the one that galls that must be heard. No idea is so repugnant that it must not be advocated. If we are not free to speak heresy and utter awful thoughts, we are not free at all. And if we are unwilling to hear

115

that with which we most violently disagree, we are not free at all. And if we are unwilling to hear that with which we most violently disagree, we are no longer citizens but have become part of the mob.

Threatening Freedom

To deny free speech in order to engineer social change in the name of accomplishing a greater good for one sector of our society erodes the freedoms of all [and] . . . threatens tryanny and injustices for those subjected to the rule of such laws.

Sarah Evans Barker, quoted in *The Christian Science Monitor*, October 10, 1985.

Nowhere is the willingness to listen more important than at a university, and nowhere is our failure more apparent than at the university whose faculty members or students think that it's legitimate to parade their own moral or political purity by shouting down the unpopular view of the day.

It will not be a week, and certainly not a month, before you will become aware that someone in your own circle of influence is saying something or thinking something very wrong. I think you have to do something about that. I think you have to help them be heard. I think you are required to listen.

5

"The First Amendment . . . does [not] extend to unrestricted license for the rock industry to pump sewage into the minds of young people."

Artistic Speech Must Be Regulated by Ethics

Charles Colson

Charles Colson, an active political figure until the Watergate Scandal of the 1970s, rededicated himself to Christian values while serving time in prison. A prolific speaker and writer, Colson believes that ethical considerations must guide society's response to artistic expression. In the following viewpoint, he writes specifically about the controversy over the impact of rock music and other popular culture on young people.

As you read, consider the following questions:

1. What does Colson think is the function of art?
2. Why does Colson believe that getting rid of certain dangerous or offensive kinds of "art" is not censorship?

Charles Colson, "Is Art Above Ethics?" Copyright 1986. Reprinted from *Christianity Today*, February 26, 1986, by permission of Fellowship Communications.

There I was, privy to one of the great struggles of the modern age. The arena was my TV set, and in it were not Reagan and Gorbachev, nor Chrysler and the UAW [United Auto Workers], but two unlikely combatants: Susan Baker, wife of the treasury secretary, wearing a choker of pearls, a dark dress, and her hair swept into a bun; and her opposition, rock star Dee Snider, attired in leather, with kinky brown, black, and blond hair cascading down his back.

Before packed congressional committee hearings, Baker spoke for a group of Washington mothers alarmed about rock lyrics that promote obscenity, violence, drugs, and the occult.

Snider testified as a performer alarmed about censorship; he was followed by others invoking that hallowed American privilege, the First Amendment. "It's really an issue of rights," one rock star sniffed. "As an artist, I have a right to self-expression."

Not a Blank Check

It may be unpopular to say this nowadays, but the First Amendment is not a blank check. As Justice Holmes wrote, the right of free speech does not extend to shouting "Fire!" in a crowded theater. Nor, I submit, does it extend to unrestricted license for the rock industry to pump sewage into the minds of young people.

But artists' rights and consumer censorship are merely surface issues. This controversy raises deeper questions.

For instance, what is art, anyway? And what does its role in our society tell us about how we value human dignity and the worth of the individual?

Historically, art has been man's creative effort to explore, ennoble, and transcend his human experience. Classically, it was created within a context that assumed the objective nature of beauty. Certain absolutes were accepted not only for man, morality, and the universe, but also for the art that mirrored them.

For the Christian, art is a manifestation of a person's creative gifts. As the heavens proclaim the glory of God, so might man's handiwork glorify him as well. And art offers not only a means to extol the Creator, but to explore the predicaments of his highest creation. It is self-expression, yes, but it does not exist as an end in itself.

Our culture today, however, regards just about anything, from subway graffiti to rock videos, as art. Indeed, many seem to believe that labeling something art automatically makes it sacrosanct, above moral judgments. Some even treat it idolatrously, like those cited by *Newsweek* who "expect art to supply some of the meaning once found elsewhere—in religion, for example."

But Christians cannot allow art to escape moral and aesthetic judgments. Nor should we allow ourselves to be portrayed as censors: If a musician can summon no more than obscenities to his performances, we must reject his work as fallen art, an adversarial expression seeking to tear down and destroy rather than build up and redeem.

Art vs. Moral Judgment

This is the heart of the issue: if society elevates art above moral judgment, then it will also consider protecting art its supreme duty.

The record producers have made this very point.

Clive Davis, president of Arista Records, conceded on "The Today Show" that lyrics extolling incest, for example, are offensive. But, he countered, "We, as the guardian of our artists and original talent, have to be very careful of . . . the creative talent that [is] the backbone and the essence of what we're all here to protect."

Davis concluded, "An artist like Prince who is today's musical creative genius is no different, perhaps, than James Joyce was to his generation. . . ."

Prince, of course, is the self-proclaimed messianic performer who, depending on his mood, will sing about the crucifixion of Christ, undress, or act out masturbation scenes on stage.

So the great contribution of this "musical genius" is supreme; never mind if the price is a bit of blasphemy here or there, or a few thousands kids led astray.

Jack Ohman, *The Oregonian*, reprinted with permission.

The ultimate consequences of this attitude can be tragic. Several years ago author Norman Mailer "felt all the awe one knows before a phenomenon" when he read the letters of imprisoned killer Jack Abbott. Mailer campaigned for Abbott's release; he was paroled to the open arms of the New York literati. Abbott's book, *In the Belly of the Beast,* an angry antiestablishment diatribe, was hailed by critics.

But it took Abbott only a few weeks of freedom before he again acted out the violence his writing extolled, brutally murdering a young waiter.

Quoted on "60 Minutes," Norman Mailer defended his efforts to have Abbott freed: "Yes, I'm willing to gamble with the safety of certain elements of society to save this man's talent."

Corruption vs. Ethics

So to Mailer, perhaps a murder here or there is worth the preservation of Abbott's art. The rock producers who consider the corrupting influence of performers like Prince a fair price to pay to protect their art are offering us the same argument: Art itself is more important than an individual's life or dignity.

Happily, the parents' confrontation with the rock industry has resulted in the agreement of 22 record companies to put warning labels on offensive albums. But that small concession does not signal victory in the larger contest. The issue is not just one of a clash of generations. Rather, it is a clash of world views.

As C.S. Lewis wrote, "If individuals live only 70 years, then a state, or a nation, or a civilization, which may last for a thousand years, is more important than an individual. But if Christianity is true, then the individual is more important, for he is everlasting and the life of a state or civilization, compared with his, is only a moment."

The choice before us is clear: Do we place our values in the primacy of art and the self-expression of the culture, or in the eternal worth of the individual created in the image of God?

As Lewis says, it all depends on whether Christianity is true or not.

6

"In music, it's still possible for an artist to speak with relative freedom, to give a voice to people and causes the political mainsteam would rather not hear from."

Artistic Speech Should Not Be Regulated

Steve Perry

Steve Perry, a rock music critic in Minneapolis, believes that it is wrong and dangerous to attempt to regulate music because of its supposedly offensive content. In the following viewpoint, he argues that the current move toward labeling or censoring music is dangerously similar to the McCarthy anti-communism craze of the 1950s.

As you read, consider the following questions:

1. Perry believes that the current movement toward labeling rock music to identify potentially offensive lyrics will lead inevitably to self-censorship. Why does he think that self-censorship is as dangerous as censorship imposed by the state?
2. What dangers does Perry see in "proscribing . . . *any* cultural expression"?
3. According to Perry, what is it that is actually feared by those who want to regulate rock and roll?

Steven Perry, "Censoring the Arts." From the November 27-December 10, 1985 issue of *In These Times*, 1300 W. Belmont, Chicago, IL 60657, (312) 472-5700. Published weekly, annual subscription: $34.95.

121

If you want to understand the current '50s-style congressional "inquiries" into the contents of popular music, you need to look past the ostensible subjects: past Madonna's lacy underthings, past the outrageous lyrics of obscure heavy metal bands, past the mindless sensationalism of the *People* magazine article that implied the Night Stalker killings were caused by the suspect's affinity for AC/DC. You need to look to things like the Artists United Against Apartheid's "Sun City" video, the single most moving display of political commitment and solidarity the rock music community has yet produced.

Or to the words with which Bruce Springsteen introduced Edwin Starr's "War" at the Los Angeles concerts that closed his tour: "When you grew up in the '60s, you grew up with the war your country was involved in every night on television. I remember a friend of mine, a drummer, would come over to my house with his Marine uniform on, saying he was going to Vietnam, and he didn't even know where it was. And we're all kinda laughing about it.

"I'd like to do this next song for you because if you're 17 or 18 out there, the next time they're gonna be looking at you, and you're gonna need a lot more information before you're gonna be able to make a decision about what's right for you to do. And blind faith in 1985 . . . your leaders will get you killed."

Pressure Toward Self-Censorship

It's no coincidence that pressure toward self-censorship in the music industry—which started with the PTA and gained clout with the formation of the Parents Music Resource Center (PMRC) by a group of congressmen's wives—has peaked in a year when political activity among rock musicians is at an all-time high. The actions of these groups don't represent an avowed conspiracy against musical activism so much as a generalized fear of rock's growing visibility and potency.

That's not to say that their political agenda is benign. Far from it. Beyond the explicit language warning tags that the two sides have settled on for the time being, the PMRC has called for a comprehensive rating scheme that would include such designations as X (profane, violent or sexually explicit lyrics), D/A (lyrics glorifying drugs or alcohol) and O (lyrics pertaining to the occult).

If the censorship potential inherent in such a system isn't immediately apparent, the response of the industry makes it clear. Camelot, the nation's second largest retail music chain, announced that carrying R- or X-rated records would cost it shops their leases. The response of Recording Industry Association of America (RIAA) President Stanley Gortikov is even more chilling. In a memo to the RIAA board of directors quoted by Dave Marsh in his Village Voice account of the controversy, Gortikov said: "It is impossible to justify publicly some of the blatant and extreme recording examples protested by the parent groups. I recommend that a renewed policy of sensitivity, discretion and reasonableness be applied in recording and releasing practices. . . . *Artist contracts, new and old, might be examined to assure that future content makes such company discretion possible"* (emphasis added).

Protecting Ignorance

There have always been foolish protests against pop culture for not being what it is—refined or reticent or subtle. Such protests are, of course, constitutionally protected. But censorship of sexually explicit expression—in high art or rock music—invariably affects literature and the arts, communication and entertainment, education and intellectual inquiry. Censorship protects only ignorance.

Leanne Katz, *USA Today*, June 5, 1987.

That veiled threat of blacklisting is a logical extension of the PMRC's current demands. And once the mechanisms of censorship (self-imposed or not) and blacklisting are in place, it isn't too hard to imagine the kind of quicksand politically-motivated artists will be standing on.

As John Cougar Mellencamp put it, "Right now, it's sex and violence; before long it'll be 'That's just too political.' That's the way it started in the '50s, with the blacklisting of actors and actresses."

Echoes of McCarthyism

For the left, any residual sympathy with PMRC's anti-sexism and violence rhetoric ought to be more than tempered by the stench of McCarthyism that wafts through the proceedings, not to mention the broader history of First Amendment infringements, which have always hurt the left far more than the right. Now, as then, qualified capitulation to the forces of censure and censorship threatens to avalanche into an unqualified sellout.

At the dawn of the McCarthy era, remember, Harry Truman had no doubt the anti-Communist movement could be contained. Thus he tacitly supported the first wave of red-baiting in the hope that it would neutralize Henry Wallace and the Democratic left and free up the mainstream for his centrist policies (especially his foreign policies, which required a measure of Russophobia in Congress and the public). When it became apparent that McCarthy wasn't content to stop there, Truman tried to choke off the Red Scare juggernaut. But by that time it was too late; he had already done his part to legitimize McCarthy's program and his administration could only scramble—unsuccessfully—to stay out of its ever-widening path.

Gortikov & Co. unwittingly play a similar role, toward similarly self-interested ends. The RIAA president wants most of all not to jeopardize pending legislation on record industry piracy and taxation of blank tape, and he's willing to sell off artists and chunks of the First Amendment to preserve that economic interest.

The '50s experience is rife with frightening lessons about the consequences of proscribing cultural expression—*any* cultural expression—in politically extreme times. Beyond blacklisting *per se*, McCarthyism claimed many victims in the same way that opponents of rock now propose to: by getting the entertainment industry to adopt a self-policed ethic of fear and conservatism.

Sometimes this took the form of industry ratings codes, such as the Comics Code—which led to the collapse of EC, the most important, controversial comics line of that era—and sometimes it was simply understood. Worse, the impact of self-censorship wasn't limited to established popular arts like movies, comics and fiction—or even to that era alone. In *Tube of Plenty*, Erik Barnouw shows how television's birth during the McCarthy era helped establish a narrative conservatism that still endures almost 40 years later.

Attack on Freedom of Expression

The compromise settlement, in which the industry agreed to print lyrics *or* attach a generic warning label, might make it appear that the battle is over. But so long as rock activists continue to make their presence felt, the pressure toward censorship isn't likely to cease. Fueled by the November 1 partial victory, PMRC member Ruth Frenzel told a reporter that it's a step in the right direction, then added, "This isn't the end of the action."

The attack on freedom of artistic expression is starting with rock because that's where the action is. Rock is the medium that speaks most directly and powerfully to the outclasses in '80s America, as well as the one that offers the greatest combination of autonomy and exposure to popular artists. The economics of film and TV production help ensure that hot subjects and views are treated conservatively, if at all—which is one big reason that record "ratings" don't have the same implications as film ratings. Try to imagine a TV drama as honest about Vietnam as "Born in the USA." It would never be aired.

But in music, it's still possible for an artist to speak with relative freedom, to give a voice to people and causes the political mainstream would rather not hear from. And that freedom is the real center of the current controversy.

Distinguishing Between Fact and Opinion

This activity is designed to help develop the basic reading and thinking skill of distinguishing between fact and opinion. Consider the following statement: "The First Amendment states that 'Congress shall make no law.... Abridging the freedom of speech.'" This is a factual statement that can be proved simply by checking the Bill of Rights in an almanac, government reference book, or encyclopedia. The following statement, however, is an opinion: "Allowing 'speech' such as pornography to be silenced is only a step away from the silencing of other unpopular 'speech' such as political opinions." This view is only one perspective from the hotly debated issue of exactly how much and what kinds of expression the First Amendment actually protects. There is no sound way to prove it true or false.

When investigating controversial issues it is important that one be able to distinguish between statements of fact and statements of opinion. It is also important to recognize that not all statements of fact are true. They may appear to be true, but some are based on inaccurate or false information. For this activity, however, we are concerned with understanding the difference between those statements which appear to be factual and those which appear to be based primarily on opinion.

Most of the following statements are taken from the viewpoints in this chapter. Consider each statement carefully. *Mark O for any statement you believe is an opinion or interpretation of facts. Mark F for any statement you believe is a fact. Mark I for any statement you believe is impossible to judge.*

If you are doing this activity as a member of a class or group, compare your answers with those of other class or group members. Be able to defend your answers. You may discover that others come to different conclusions than you do. Listening to the reasons others present for their answers may give you valuable insights in distinguishing between fact and opinion.

O = *opinion*
F = *fact*
I = *impossible to judge*

125

1. The author is profoundly wrong in suggesting that speech that diverges widely from community values should not be tolerated.

2. The First Amendment protects the right to speak and to publish.

3. It is best to tolerate even the most obnoxious and offensive ideas.

4. As we come closer and closer to true democracy, we are ever more susceptible to a certain kind of mob rule in which popularity substitutes for principle and consensus is mistaken for wisdom.

5. It is the law in this country that the individual has a definite right to personal expression.

6. Allowing individuals to hear and assess the views of others is no guarantee that they will always make wise decisions.

7. Communication helps us develop the human capacities of rational thought, moral judgment, and emotional attachment.

8. I do not believe there is a point at which individual freedom must surrender to the pressing needs of the community.

9. Even a false idea or, for that matter, an evil idea can serve the cause of truth if it is subjected to rational criticism.

10. Literature and the arts appeal more to the imagination and the emotions than they do to reason.

11. The attack on freedom of artistic expression is starting with rock because that's where the action is; rock is the medium that speaks most directly and powerfully to the outclasses in '80s America.

12. *Time* magazine reported that some newspapers published pictures of the head of an out-of-favor princess superimposed on photos of nude bodies in obscene poses.

13. The First Amendment was not written for a nation made up exclusively of ladies and gentlemen, and it protects a large range of expressions that are neither refined nor elegant.

Periodical Bibliography

The following articles have been selected to supplement the diverse views presented in this chapter.

Norman Dorsen	"Liberty or License: Can Free Speech Become Too Costly?" *Civil Liberties*, Summer/Fall 1986. Available from ACLU, 132 W. 43rd St., New York, NY 10036.
Margaret Anne Gallagher	"A Tyranny of Pity," *National Review*, September 26, 1986.
Eric Gelman et al.	"MTV's Message," *Newsweek*, December 30, 1985.
Virginia Held	"Free Expression," *Society* September/October 1984.
Nat Hentoff	"The Silencers Among Us," *The Progressive*, July 1984.
Abbie Hoffman	"Closing Argument," *The Nation*, May 2, 1987.
Norma Klein	"Being Banned," *SIECUS Report*, July 1985. Available from SIECUS, New York University, 32 Washington Place, New York, NY 10003.
Erwin Kroll	"Bookburners," *The Progressive*, December 1985.
Jethro Lieberman	"Freedom of Expression: Lessons from the Constitution," *Wilson Library Bulletin*, April 1987.
Judy Mathewson	"Porn: Does It Deserve First Amendment Protection?" *Common Cause Magazine*, September/October 1986. Available from Common Cause, 2030 M Street NW, Washington, DC 20036.
Media & Values	Issue focusing on "Violence and Sexual Violence in the Media," Fall 1985. Available from Media & Values, 1962 South Shenandoah, Los Angeles, CA 90034.
Charley Reese	"Local Issue: School Reading Lists," *Conservative Chronicle*, July 22, 1987. Available from Conservative Chronicle, 9 Second Street NW, Hampton, IA 50441.

Phyllis Schlafly	Four brief articles against pornography, *The Phyllis Schlafly Report*, April 1987. Available from The Eagle Trust Fund, Box 618, Alton, IL 62002.
Society	Special section on "Pornography and Its Discontents," July/August 1987.
Kurt Vonnegut Jr.	"The Idea Killers," *Playboy*, January 1984.
George F. Will	"Fine-Tuning from the Bench," *Newsweek*, July 21, 1986.
Steven Wishnia	"Rockin' with the First Amendment," *The Nation*, October 24, 1987.

What Violates the Right to Privacy?

Chapter Preface

Initially, the Fourth Amendment to the Constitution was created by American revolutionaries who had suffered from intrusive violations by British troops. Early American leaders created the Fourth Amendment to insure "the right of the people to be secure in their persons, homes, papers, and effects, against unreasonable searches and seizures." Since the turn of the twentieth century, however, the interpretation of the Fourth Amendment has been broadened to a more general concept of individual right to privacy. The courts began to recognize this concept when technological advances such as cameras and electronic listening devices made the issue of privacy more complicated.

The controversial nature of the right to privacy arises from differing definitions of "unreasonable searches and seizures." Is the request for a blood or urine sample an unreasonable search? Does the state have a right to dictate sexual practices between consenting adults? Can employers randomly test employees for drug use?

Because the notion of an individual's right to privacy is so new and technology's intrusion on this right so inevitable, the courts seem fated to continue struggling with cases related to this issue. The viewpoints in this chapter present various views on how far the right to privacy should extend.

> *"If we choose to violate the rights of the innocent in order to discover and act against the guilty, then we have transformed our country into a police state."*

Drug Testing Violates the Right to Privacy

Abbie Hoffman

Abbie Hoffman is a political activist who rose to fame during the social turmoil of the 1960s. Hoffman's causes include ending US involvement in Central America, halting CIA recruitment on college campuses, and preserving the environment. In the following viewpoint, Hoffman argues that indiscriminate drug testing violates employees' civil liberties. He maintains that urine testing is a needless invasion of privacy that must be stopped.

As you read, consider the following questions:

1. Why did Judge Sarokin rule that testing violated the Plainfield fire fighters' liberties?
2. Why is Hoffman frightened by the lack of governmental protection given to private employees?
3. What does the author suggest people do to protest drug tests?

On May 26, 1986, Memorial Day, the city of Plainfield, New Jersey, inspired by the War on Drugs, launched a dawn attack on its own fire department.

At 6:30 A.M., the Plainfield fire chief, the director of public affairs, and a small battalion of Bladder Cops burst into the city firehouse, bolted all exits, woke everyone up, and announced, "Rise and shine!" A surprise urine test was about to begin.

One by one, each worker present was led into the fire chief's office and ordered to submit a urine sample under the direct observation of hired voyeurs. Some protested. Months later, fireman Fulton Allen, on PBS's public-affairs program "Currents," recalled, "When I went to take my urinalysis, they had a guy in there with me. I never saw this guy before, and I couldn't urinate with somebody watching. So he said, 'I'll turn my back.' I said, 'No, what are you, gay?' This is how I felt!" Allen threw his hands up in a combination of despair and disbelief.

Objections by the fire fighters were overruled on the spot, and the city extracted what it wanted. Each urine sample was carefully labeled, sealed, and shipped off for drug evaluation.

Trapped and Tested

Flush with victory, the city decided to strike again. Twice more, on May 28 and June 12, urine troopers raided the same station, on different shifts, until virtually all 103 workers had been trapped and tested. Those who refused were threatened. "I felt that my rights were being violated," said Cecil Allen, another fire fighter. "I didn't see any reason why I had to give this urine test. But according to the city, I either had to give the urine test or be suspended. . . . I felt totally violated."

While both city officials and fire fighters awaited the next strike, the atmosphere at the station house grew tense. No one was sure exactly what or who was going to go down. And then, as mysteriously as they had begun, the raids stopped. A few weeks passed, the fire fighters thought the issue was dead, and no one was any the worse. They were happy to join with millions of their fellow Americans in celebrating Liberty Week. The fire fighters offered silent thanks to the great Statue Goddess in the harbor that their bladders hadn't turned them in. "Thank you, great Lady of the Light," they murmured, as the sky above their heads exploded with 3 million dollars' worth of fireworks.

Suddenly, the light went out. Between July 10 and July 14, sixteen workers were notified that their urine had tested positive for "controlled dangerous substances." They were summarily terminated. No severance pay. No appeal. No confirmation testing. Nothing. They were simply out of their jobs and on the street. Laboratory results and the substances found in their urine were, as far as the Firehouse 16 were concerned, classified information.

As if losing their jobs wasn't enough, ten days later they were charged with "commission of a criminal act," and informed that legal action against them was pending. Miller Time this was not.

Striking back, the Firehouse 16 sued (*Ben Capua et al.* vs. *City of Plainfield*). U.S. District Judge H. Lee Sarokin was impressed enough with the complaint to issue a temporary restraining order. He ordered a halt to all drug testing (the city had already started in on the police department), and reinstated those who had been fired.

The Right To Be Left Alone

If you don't use drugs, you have nothing to hide. Why object to testing?

Innocent people do have something to hide: their privacy. This "right to be left alone" is, in the words of the eminent Supreme Court Justice Louis Brandeis, "the most comprehensive of rights and the right most valued by civilized men." Urine tests are an unprecedented invasion of privacy. In order to guard against specimen tampering, it is standard practice to require employees to urinate in the presence of a witness, which, in the words of one judge, is "an experience which even if courteously supervised can be humiliating and degrading."

The American Civil Liberties Union, *ACLU Speaks Out!* March 1987.

Harold Gibson, Director of Public Safety for Plainfield, claimed responsibility for the whole operation. "The fire fighters were not the enemy," he explained to the PBS audience. "I'd be the first to admit that. However, in determining who the enemy was in this particular set of circumstances, it was necessary to put everybody through the metal detector, so to speak. And that's what we did.

"We, as administrators, should be allowed to impinge on those Constitutional rights in order to accomplish the objective of determining whether they're drug abusers or not," he finished.

A Violation of Rights

At the subsequent trial, Judge Sarokin held that the discharged workers' expectations of privacy were severely compromised by random compulsory urinalysis:

> The sweeping manner which the [officials] set about to accomplish their goals violated the fire fighters' individual liberties. The search was unreasonable because defendants [the city] lacked any suspicion as to that [individual] fire fighter. . . . The invidious effect of such mass, round-up urinalysis is that it casually sweeps up the innocent with the guilty and willingly sacrifices each individual's Fourth Amendment right in the name

133

of some larger public interest. The City of Plainfield essentially presumed the guilt of each person tested.

The Court ruled for the discharged fire fighters. They were permanently reinstated, with back pay. The Judge's rebuke was a strong legal blow to urine testing. He did not mince words:

> We would be appalled at the specter of the police spying on employees during their free time and then reporting their activities to their employers. Drug testing is a form of surveillance, albeit a technological one. Nonetheless it reports on a person's off-duty activities just as surely as if someone had been present and watching. It is George Orwell's 'Big Brother' Society come to life.

Judge Sarokin added:

> If we choose to violate the rights of the innocent in order to discover and act against the guilty, then we have transformed our country into a police state and abandoned one of the fundamental tenets of our free society. In order to win the war against drugs, we must not sacrifice the life of the Constitution in the battle.

The city of Plainfield grudgingly reinstated the workers and did not appeal the decision. As strong as Judge Sarokin's ruling was, it should be noted that it attacked only the *circumstances* surrounding urine testing. It did not rule that the procedure in and of itself is unconstitutional. The Court of Appeals was not asked to review judgment. The District Court's findings are narrowly limited to this single incident, and possibly to others involving random, compulsory screening in the judge's district. . . .

"Public Safety"

Two factors—a search's reasonability and public safety concerns—have been the focus of additional appellate court decisions. *McDonell et al.* vs. *Hunter*, in the Eighth Circuit Court of Appeals, concerns prison guards in Iowa who brought suit to invalidate what they considered persecution, that is, urine testing precipitated by an unsubstantiated letter accusing several guards of keeping "improper" company. The U.S. District Court judge found for the plantiffs; the procedure was an unreasonable search under the Fourth Amendment, lacking probable cause, standards, and specificity. Civil libertarians breathed again.

But on January 12, 1987, the Federal Appeals Court for Iowa reversed *McDonell*, declaring "the need to maintain prison discipline and security justifies urinalysis. . . . Reasonable suspicion to test any employees exists within prison property by virtue of the criminal atmosphere." Public safety is placed above the guards' reasonable expectation to privacy. . . .

With respect to "public safety," the broadest range of occupations seems to be accepted. Just think for a minute about the variety of occupations that relate to your own "public safety." Construction workers, elevator operators, electricians, drivers, sports fans, pharmacists, rock bands that show up three hours late for concerts, hospital personnel, hang gliders. You get the idea. An argument could be made for just about any occupation.

Not all matters in the court system are determined by formal suit ending in final adjudication. If a party facing litigation decides not to contest the charge, a consent decree may be issued by the court, binding both parties to a mutually acceptable resolution. A few federal agencies appear so uncertain of their right to test workers that they've settled actions out of court, rather than risk judicial censure. Other agencies have accepted consent decrees. In Philadelphia on February 28, 1986, a class action was filed

By Bill Sanders, The Milwaukee Journal. © 1987 News America Syndicate, Inc.

against the U.S. Postal Service. The plaintiffs, a group of job applicants, were required to submit to urinalysis drug screening as part of the hiring process. They claimed their rejections based on positive test results were discriminatory and unconstitutional. Instead of going to trial, the U.S. Justice Department approved a consent decree requiring the Philadelphia Post Office "terminate its present policy and practice of requiring all applicants for employment to submit to urinalysis drug testing." The Post Office also promised never to test again in Philadelphia unless mandated by the Postmaster General. $5,000, priority employment, and legal fees were awarded each of the plaintiffs as partial settlement. . . .

Public vs. Private

The disparity between federal and private employees is frightening. It seems like a worker is being penalized for his or her selection of private over public workplace. Rules which prevent excessive intrusion have not kept pace with corporate growth. A company security guard faces far fewer constraints than real policemen or federal agents with respect to privacy. While underground, I once had a job in a large hotel restaurant. Every night upon leaving, each and every worker was patted down by security guards in an effort to prevent illegal steak exportation. Police, under Fourth Amendment constraints, do not have this right to pat down indiscriminately.

As companies have expanded, they have tended to assume more and more control over their workers. The Reagan battle cry of "less government" has ostensibly encouraged employer domination. When government is not anxious to control, Corporate America is only too happy to step in. If companies want to weed out undesirables with urine tests, the Reagan Administration stands ready to hold the cup.

Despite limited protections, a handful of suits have been filed in the private sector. All are based on violations of state privacy laws. The cost of litigation is prohibitive to most workers. Legal organizations recruit victimized employees, in the hopes of establishing precedent cases that may ultimately protect others. Often, litigation is the only chance a penalized worker has to gain reinstatement and/or restitution. As of this writing, no final decisions in private sector cases have been given. Challenges are too recent. However, a few pending actions are worth noting for the promise they hold.

Jennings et al. vs. *Minco Technology Labs.* Brenda Jennings, a gutsy Texan, brought a class action suit challenging the legality of Minco Labs' mandatory, mass urinalysis. She contends they are issued randomly, and without just cause. This violates the State of Texas Right to Privacy; the Texas right to be free from unlawful search and seizure; and due process. Among other complaints is the degrading way the tests are administered. Workers are placed under close physical surveillance while urinating, to prevent sample tampering. There's a fine line between watching someone urinate and sexual harassment. The confidential information contained in the urine "gives rise to the spectre of pretextual use for illegal job discrimination and unjust employment deprivation." Jennings contends that urine screens give the boss access to information long considered private. Ms. Jennings is seeking injunctive relief, damages, and a halt to drug screening of all Minco workers.

Private Functions

The president of Beth Israel Hospital in New York has been quoted as saying that during drug tests, someone "must watch each person urinate into a bottle. If that is not done, it's a sham." I haven't gone through the Constitution with a fine comb, but I'm sure our founding fathers wouldn't have let this nation get off the ground without putting something in there about going to the bathroom alone.

Drug tests are illegal, expensive, inaccurate, stupid—and those are their comforting aspects.

P.J. O'Rourke, *Playboy*, February 1987.

Similar charges were brought in a federal case, *Ben Capua* vs. *City of Plainfield*. Judge Sarokin ruled against the testers: forcing an employee to urinate in front of another person violated all standards of human dignity and was particularly distasteful to the court. Is it any less distasteful in the private sector?

Abuse of Testing

In closing, let me mention one of the most flagrant misuses of mass drug screening imaginable. [In 1983] the Washington, D.C. Superior Court's prison system began a urine-testing program which is so outrageous several other jail systems are, naturally, beginning to copy it. All arrestees facing *any* criminal charge and held overnight must submit to a urine test. Using EMIT screens, inmates are tested for five controlled substances—amphetamines, cocaine, opiates, methadone, and PCP. About 300 people arrested are tested every morning between 6 and 9 A.M. (the first urine of the day is the most concentrated, and therefore the most potentially damaging). The results, which take about 20 minutes to process, are used in establishing conditions of release. A positive result can affect amount of bail, conditions of bail, release on personal cognizance, and the like. *Everyone is tested*, whether the alleged crime is drug-related, murder, or civil disobedience.

The Pre-trial Services Division of the Superior Court runs the program. "There is virtually one hundred percent compliance," noted Supervisor John Carver. What happens if you refuse? "If the judge wants to, you can be held in contempt of court," he said. "If you refuse to be tested," says Washington attorney Nina Kraut, "you get no appearance before a judge. Which means no release conditions are set."

Someone has to defy the program successfully, or it will soon become common practice. Mayor Koch has recommended a similar system for New York City's Rikers Island. Anyone in jail is naturally very anxious to get out and get out quickly. Giving up Constitutional rights along with some urine seems minor compared to the horror of a crowded, violent jail. My last experience in the D.C. jail was memorable. I was arrested for wearing a shirt that resembled the American flag, while protesting being hauled before the House Un-American Activities Committee. The news, without telling of the details, claimed it was "desecration of the flag." The guards assumed that I had burned Old Glory. In jail, refusing to give a blood sample, they pinned me to the floor and jabbed in the needle. Eight weeks to the day, I came down with serum hepatitis. It was a type transmitted only through infected needles, with a two-month incubation period. I was convinced the guards had infected me on purpose. A subsequent lawsuit proved unsuccessful, but did reveal an extraordinarily high rate of serum hepatitis in that rotten D.C. jail. Someone—maybe me if arrested protesting government policy in a demonstration—has to just say no to the D.C. jailer. Lawyers cannot go to court without clients.

Fighting urine tests is lonely work, carried out in dark places. But someone's got to do it!

"Courts thus far have failed to find that testing
constitutes an invasion of privacy where the
employer reasonably suspects drug or alcohol
use."

Drug Testing Does Not Necessarily Violate the Right to Privacy

Melissa Skidmore Cowan

Most constitutional lawyers agree that the right to privacy is not
absolute. However, many disagree on how best to maintain the
delicate balance between the state's interest and personal freedom.
In the following viewpoint, Melissa Skidmore Cowan, a contributing editor to the *Cincinnati Law Review*, writes that US courts
have supported drug testing in cases where probable cause has
been established. Cowan argues that the cost of drug abuse to
society legitimizes the involuntary testing of certain employees.

As you read, consider the following questions:

1. Why does Skidmore argue that drug tests are not
   "unreasonable searches and seizures"?
2. According to the author, do private employers need
   reasonable suspicion before testing? Why or why not?
3. In Skidmore's opinion, why are high risk employees not
   covered by the equal protection clause?

Melissa Skidmore Cowan, "Workers, Drinks, and Drugs: Can Employers Test?"
Cincinnati Law Review, vol. 55, no. 1, 1986. Reprinted with permission.

Although alcohol and drug abuse in the workplace is not a new problem, an awareness of its magnitude and consequences has developed only recently. Employee drug use has become a crisis for American business, costing industry as much as sixty billion dollars every year. Absenteeism, medical claims, and reduced productivity are only some of the resulting costs. There is also a growing risk to the safety of the public, as well as to other employees. Heightened awareness of the problem has caused employers to implement drug and alcohol testing to discover abusers and thereby to reduce costs and risks. Although the transportation industry especially has been concerned with detecting and eliminating drug and alcohol abuse, nearly fifty percent of the Fortune 500 companies have implemented or are considering drug screening.

As drug and alcohol testing becomes more widespread, employees and commentators question its legality. The ability to prevent testing, however, may depend on whether the employee is part of the private or public sector. Only public employees clearly have a right to challenge testing as a violation of their constitutional rights because state action is lacking in the private sector employment relationship. Courts, however, have been increasingly willing to impose constitutional restrictions on private employers.

Because drug and alcohol testing is a fairly recent development, legal constraints are just beginning to evolve as employees test the legality of workplace rules that permit screening. Although employers appear to be safe in administering tests to job applicants, the scope of their right to test employees already on the payroll is still being delineated. . . .

Not Absolute

The United States Constitution protects the right to privacy. In addition, employees may have a right to privacy under state law. Some states have laws that limit employers' rights to obtain, use, and disclose information about employees, and a number of states guarantee the right to privacy in their constitution. Also, there are common law privacy theories, such as tortious invasion of privacy and defamation. Under either state or federal law, however, the right to privacy is not absolute.

Determining whether the right to privacy exists under the federal Constitution requires a balancing of the employer's need for the intrusion against the employee's privacy interest. Courts have used this balancing approach where employees alleged that testing violated their right to privacy under the fourth amendment. Because an individual has a reasonable expectation of privacy in the information contained in his body, it is generally accepted that blood, breath, and urine tests constitute searches and seizures under the fourth amendment. The fourth amendment, however, prohibits only unreasonable searches and seizures. The balancing test helps courts to determine whether drug and alcohol testing is reasonable.

In *Allen v. City of Marietta*, a Georgia federal district court concluded that urinalysis testing by a government employer was not an unreasonable search because the employee's expectation of privacy was outweighed by the employer's need to investigate employee misconduct. The court, however, limited the scope of the employer's right to test by stating that the employer must be investigating misconduct directly related to the employee's performance of duties. Where an employer was using drug tests to investigate criminal misconduct, the search would become unreasonable under the fourth amendment. According to the court, testing was proper in this case because the employer had administered the tests solely to determine whether several employees were using drugs that would affect their ability to perform their jobs properly.

The Need for Sacrifice

Civil liberties are extremely important, and we don't want to lose them. However, some sacrifice of basic rights is the price that must be paid for the privilege of living closely together while maintaining law and order. Drugs are illegal, and society must have the ability to protect itself.

US citizens have already agreed to invasion of privacy, and to limit free speech. Baggage and passengers must pass through metal detectors before people board aircraft. No one may joke about carrying guns when he passes through security to board an airplane, or yell "Fire!" in a crowded auditorium.

Ralph Duniway, *The Christian Science Monitor,* May 1, 1986.

Where safety is involved, most courts have been quick to find that testing by a public employer is reasonable under the fourth amendment. These courts have reasoned that individuals employed in jobs that affect public safety have a lesser expectation of privacy. Weighing this privacy interest against the significant interest employers have in limiting the extreme risks created by drug and alcohol use in these jobs, testing does not appear to be an unreasonable intrusion.

Protecting the Public

Employing this reasoning, the District of Columbia Court of Appeals upheld drug testing of police officers in *Turner v. Fraternal Order of Police*. Recognizing the potential dangers created by police drug use, the court viewed testing as a means to protect the public by ensuring that officers are fit to perform their jobs. Because the public interest in safety outweighed the officer's privacy interest, the court found no fourth amendment violation.

The right to privacy under the fourteenth amendment is also subject to a balancing of competing interests. In *Shoemaker v. Handel* a New Jersey federal district court employed this balancing approach to determine whether drug and alcohol testing violated the privacy rights protected by the fourteenth amendment. Jockeys in that case alleged that drug testing violated their privacy rights because it compelled the disclosure of personal information and did not ensure the confidentiality of the information obtained. The court, however, determined that the state's interest in the information outweighed the employees' privacy interest based on three grounds. First, the state had a substantial interest in strictly regulating horse racing to ensure its safety, and the disclosure of medical information narrowly furthered that interest. Second, the testing regulations provided for the strict confidentiality of the information obtained. Third, the tests were to be administered privately. Consequently, the court held that the jockeys did not have a valid claim for invasion of privacy under the fourteenth amendment.

As with federal law, the right to privacy under state law does not extend to all situations in which an individual's privacy is affected. Under most states' laws, an individual can state a cause of action for tortious invasion of privacy by showing that his private affairs were publicized or by showing that someone intruded into his private affairs in such a manner as to outrage a reasonable man of ordinary sensibilities. However, where drug and alcohol testing is conducted confidentially and for a legitimate business purpose, courts may be reluctant to find an invasion of privacy. . . .

Reasonable Suspicion

Courts and arbitrators have placed some limitations on the implementation of drug and alcohol testing. Most authorities, for example, have required employers to reasonably suspect an employee of drug or alcohol use before administering a test. In analyzing the claims of private employees, arbitrators consistently have examined whether the employer had a reasonable basis for requesting that the employee take a sobriety test. In *Wabco* the arbitrator ruled that a private employee had an obligation to take a drug test because the employer had objective facts suggesting that the employee was under the influence. There is no constitutional restriction on private employers, however, that requires them to have a reasonable suspicion before testing.

In contrast, many courts and arbitrators have required explicitly

Mike Lukavich for the New Orleans Times-Picayune. Reprinted with permission.

that public employers reasonably suspect drug or alcohol use before testing because government entities are subject to the strictures of the fourth amendment. It appears that the public employer need not have probable cause to conduct testing, but he must be able to point to objective facts that justify testing and rational inferences that can be drawn from those facts in light of experience. Requiring employers to have a reasonable suspicion prevents an unreasonable invasion of the employee's legitimate expectation of privacy. . . .

Equal Protection

Courts and arbitrators have declined to use the equal protection clause of the fourteenth amendment to limit drug and alcohol testing by employers where the testing policy has been applied consistently to all employees. Because neither alcoholics nor drug addicts are a suspect class, to avoid an equal protection violation a public employer need show only a rational basis for treating substance abusing employees differently than other employees. In *In re Springfield Mass Transit District* a union contended that the singling out of one employee for testing violated the equal protection clause. The arbitrator, however, concluded that the employer had shown a rational basis for treating that employee differently. Because the employee was suspected of being intoxicated, he was set apart from his co-workers and could not claim he had been denied equal protection.

Moreover, one court has held that testing employees who perform high risk jobs more frequently than other employees does not constitute an equal protection violation. In *Shoemaker v. Handel* the court found no denial of equal protection although the regulations and procedures of the New Jersey Racing Commission provided for more frequent testing of jockeys than other employees. The court reasoned that the testing program bore a rational relationship to the legitimate state purpose of preventing racetrack accidents. . . .

Alternative Methods

Employers must weigh the benefits of random testing against the likelihood that courts or legislatures will prohibit testing in the absence of individualized suspicion. Employers who do not wish to risk liability for randomly testing employees have several alternatives. First, courts generally have upheld drug and alcohol testing as part of a routine physical examination. Thus, employers can achieve some of the benefits of random testing by not notifying employees of the date of the examination in advance. The problem with this alternative is that it limits the number of times an employee can be tested randomly. An employer probably will be able to conduct physical exams annually only. A second alternative is to monitor work performance carefully. Supervisors should be trained to detect the first signs of drug and alcohol use. In addition, supervisors should keep track of absences, tardiness, and accidents to alert them of possible substance abuse. The facts learned through careful monitoring could establish the reasonable suspicion necessary for testing. Third, employers can hire private detectives. The information gained about employee work habits could establish a reasonable suspicion of drug or alcohol use or might provide sufficient evidence of drug or alcohol use so that testing would be unnecessary. Employers will have to evaluate these alternatives to random testing in light of the specific interests of their business.

Although courts thus far have failed to find that testing constitutes an invasion of privacy where the employer reasonably suspects drug or alcohol use, commentators still question the legality of testing on this basis. Because of the paucity of case law on this issue, employers should be concerned that an employee could challenge testing successfully. Employers, however, can take precautions to avoid liability for invasion of privacy. First, employers should communicate their testing policy clearly to employees. Although notice of testing may not constitute a waiver of constitutional rights, it does lessen an employee's expectation of privacy. Second, employers should maintain the confidentiality of test results. Where only a few key supervisors know that an employee tested positively, it is much more difficult for an employee to claim that his privacy was invaded significantly. Finally, where employees are unionized, the employer should bargain to get a contract provision permitting testing. Although bargaining may not be mandatory, a contract clause on testing would constitute a knowing and intelligent waiver of privacy rights by employees. . . .

Interests of the Employer

Like polygraph testing and wiretapping, sobriety tests represent a collision between technology and privacy. Clearly, testing reveals many details about an employee's private life unrelated to job performance. Conducted properly, however, it is the best method of uncovering drug and alcohol abuse by workers. Resolution of this confrontation requires balancing the civil liberties of the individual against the interests of the employer.

Drugs Are Not Protected

Opponents of drug screening programs argue that testing infringes upon an individual's right to privacy. That position is based on an implied right under the Constitution. Yet courts have held that the use or possession of illegal substances is not protected by a constitutional right of privacy.

Neil J. Adkins, *California Business*, August 1986.

Thus far, courts generally have found the interest of the employer to be more significant. Drug and alcohol abuse is exacting enormous economic costs from business. More important in the courts' balancing, however, are the substantial safety risks presented by substance abuse on the job. Nevertheless, the willingness of courts to permit testing by employers will diminish if employers do not ensure the reliability of test results. There is no reason to allow technological invasions of privacy if the technology is ineffective.

"It would be a violation of our rights if social and scientific researchers could intrude into our private lives without our knowledge or consent."

Mandatory AIDS Testing Violates the Right to Privacy

Bill Griffin

Many civil libertarians believe that singling out a group of people for disease testing is discriminatory and an intrusion by the state. Since no cure for AIDS has been found, they argue, the violation of privacy is not justified by concern for public health. In the following viewpoint, Bill Griffin, a writer for *The Catholic Worker*, argues that mandatory AIDS testing will unduly stigmatize homosexuals and drug users.

As you read, consider the following questions:

1. In Griffin's opinion, how would mandatory testing undermine doctor/patient relationships?
2. When does the author believe mandatory AIDS testing will be acceptable?
3. Griffin fears how data taken from AIDS testing will be used. Why?

Bill Griffin, "Mandatory AIDS Testing Reconsidered," *The Catholic Worker*, June/July 1987. Reprinted with permission.

At the present time, among the 35,000 known victims of Acquired Immune Deficiency Syndrome (A.I.D.S.) in the United States, there have been over 20,000 deaths. The Centers for Disease Control in Atlanta projects that by 1990 there will be over 150,000 persons suffering with this fatal disease, of whom 50,000 will die by the end of that year. In the media, and in public debates there are increasing calls for mandatory blood testing for the Human Immuno-suppressive Virus (H.I.V.) which, in an as yet unknown number of cases, primarily brings on the full-blown form of the disease A.I.D.S.

H.I.V. is a primarily blood borne virus which can be present and detectable in a person's blood stream, but can lie dormant for up to fifteen years, according to some researchers. H.I.V. is known to be transmitted by the sharing of needles contaminated with blood, as takes place with intravenous drug users, and through sexual intercourse. In this country, the majority of the cases of A.I.D.S. has occurred with intravenous drug users, homosexual men and hemophiliacs who have been given tainted blood products. The number of heterosexuals, primarily women, with the disease has doubled from two to four percent of all cases within the last several years. Because it is sexually transmitted, proponents of mandatory testing for H.I.V. want it to be done in conjunction with contact tracing: spouses and the sexual partners of those who have tested positive would be located and informed, and presumably, forced to undergo the test themselves.

Ethical Implications

The intense controversy over broadening the voluntary testing that is being done at this time centers on the profound consequences such a decision will have on our civil liberties. The United States military has already ordered mandatory testing for its two million members. What will happen if all employers require testing for every employee? The ethical implications of mandatory testing need to be soberly examined.

The rationale for compulsory tests lies in the idea that persons who are told that they are carriers of the virus that can possibly lead to A.I.D.S. will refrain from high risk activities that can spread the disease. This, at least, would slow the transmission of the disease. Even if this expectation is fulfilled by only a few who test positive, "This will save hundreds of thousands of lives over the years, for the virus spreads exponentially, and every time we convince one person not to pass it on we save scores of others," writes David Carlin, a columnist for *Commonweal*.

David Carlin goes on to propose that mandatory testing begin with all current and future hospital in-patients and that it be accompanied by "counseling for all those who test positive; by imprisonment for prostitutes who continue to ply their trade after testing positive; by criminal sanctions for sero-positive persons who engage in sexual intercourse without first advising their partners of this condition, and by segregation of prison inmates who test positive." Carlin only reassures us, in an offhand manner, that all this must be done "within a framework of law guaranteeing reasonable confidentiality and protecting carriers of A.I.D.S. from discrimination in housing, employment and so forth" (*Commonweal*, April 24, 1987).

A Critique

These draconian proposals can be critiqued on three important points. First, what does recent history have to teach us about the public acceptance of this type of indiscriminate mass screening? Secondly, if such mandatory testing is blindly imposed on an ever-widening scale, what will happen to our society's traditional belief in the requirement of informed, voluntary consent as the basis for all medical procedures? Thirdly, how will the confidentiality and privacy of the individual be protected? Privacy, the right to control access to information concerning our private life and confidentiality, and knowing that information we freely give will not be revealed without our permission, are the bedrock on which the doctor-patient relationship is founded. Should medicine be encouraged or even allowed to become an extension of the police function of the state?

A Weapon of Homophobia

Test drugs, not people. Do not allow racist, homophobic, and sexist individuals to use AIDS as a weapon to eliminate their enemy. AIDS has become a passport for discrimination and injustice.

Rebecca Cole, *New York Native*, September 28, 1987.

Some recent history can shed needed light on what can be expected concretely from a mass, obligatory screening program. And it can illuminate the morality of such a policy. One attempt to implement such a plan occurred in connection with the disease sickle cell anemia. This hereditary, painful and life-shortening illness, affecting black persons almost exclusively, provoked much legislation when an effective genetic test for its presence was devised. At one point, twenty-nine states had passed mass, genetic-screening laws, most of them compulsory. Many black legislators, at the time, supported these measures with the praiseworthy goal of being able to warn two sickle-cell-trait-carrying persons, who wanted to marry, of the risks their offspring would run.

Unexpectedly, there was a very hostile response to the mandatory testing within the black community. Many were very anxious and did not fully understand the difference between being a carrier of a defective gene and having the disease, because authorities had not made the effort to provide adequate and reassuring explanations. The black community instinctively feared and correctly protested the stigmatization they felt resulted from compulsory screening.

Voluntary Consent

Eventually, more thorough and compassionate education about sickle cell anemia was provided and screening programs were put on a voluntary basis. Medical authorities concluded that, in this way, their goal of protecting the public health was most effectively achieved.

While these events do not mirror the A.I.D.S. crisis, they do show us clearly the kinds of political and social questions we face. The stigmatization of and discrimination against a tragically vulnerable minority will be the totalitarian sins our society will be tempted by and which it will have to guard against as the A.I.D.S. situation evolves.

A second critique of the inappropriately wide scale of mandatory testing has to do with the importance of informed, voluntary consent. This is recognized as the moral foundation of every medical procedure and, especially, of every medical experiment. Free and uncoerced consent was established as the basic ethical requirement for any human experimentation by the Nuremberg Code after the heinous experiments of the Nazis came to light. While the blood test for H.I.V. is now accurate and safe, it possesses no therapeutic value, here and now, for the person being tested. It can only provide knowledge that can be useful for protecting others in the future. This distinction between a therapeutic and a non-therapeutic procedure is an important one.

We do have a duty to preserve our being and to cooperate in the building up of the common good; this includes the obligation to promote the state of public health. When there is an effective, therapeutic immunization program for A.I.D.S. it will be the moral responsibility of all those in high risk groups to take part. However, since the blood test has no therapeutic value, at this time, for the individual, it can be considered, I believe, to be on the level of only an experiment to gather data. As such, the Nuremberg Code calls for participants in it to give their informed and voluntary consent.

The issue of free and knowledgeable consent contains a very important value for our humanity. Pharmaceutical companies no longer test their drugs on prisoners in our society because it is fundamentally doubted if a prisoner can really give his or her uncoerced consent. Mandatory testing for H.I.V., imposed in an arbitrary and indiscriminate fashion, would undermine this value and, as a society, we would lose something very crucial according to the Nuremberg Code.

The third and most grave criticism, given the rising levels of public fear and misinformation, that can be raised against scatter gun, compulsory testing is the short shrift given to the protection of the individual's right to privacy and confidentiality. Human beings are persons who often require help with a multitude of private matters that are not meant for public airing. We turn to our friends and to trustworthy professionals when we need to get help. It would be a violation of our rights if social and scientific researchers could intrude into our private lives without our knowledge or consent.

Public Harassment

> With the present pogromist atmosphere around AIDS anyone who tests positive would face discrimination and harassment and therefore mandatory testing will only drive people underground and away from medical institutions. Further, it has been reported in the press that the test for AIDS antibodies has a high error margin. So what this means is that people could be falsely diagnosed as having AIDS but by the time they are correctly diagnosed, they may in the meantime have lost their job, lost their insurance, been kicked out of school and generally harassed.

Revolutionary Worker, June 8, 1987.

Advocates of compulsory testing do not want to spell out in specific detail how data from their tests will be handled. Who will have access? What penalties will be imposed for misuse of information from the tests? Our country has a long and sad history of racism, which hasty advocates of widespread mandatory testing want to ignore. What kinds of cruel economic, social, and political discrimination will those who test positive for H.I.V. suffer? We must be chary, *in advance*, of the rights of the large number of those who might abruptly be branded as pariahs by any massive, mandatory blood screening plan.

The institution of any plan of this kind is an unethical course of action. Testing must remain, as it is now, a voluntary option in order to be used effectively by all those who feel they are at risk, and by medical doctors seeking to establish a diagnosis. Any broadening of testing for H.I.V. must be rational and fit into a framework of confidentiality and privacy, strictly protected from abuse. Making testing for H.I.V. part of the tests for obtaining a marriage license, if the concerns I have mentioned are adequately addressed, would be an example of the ethical broadening of testing. This would be the kind of balanced, limited and specifically targeted mandatory testing for H.I.V. that would be beneficial, and help to avoid the tragedy of infants being born with the H.I.V. virus and going on to develop A.I.D.S.

Human Rights

As a society, we must focus our efforts on many fronts. We must emphasize education and inform all as to the very real dangers of intravenous drug abuse and heterosexual and homosexual promiscuity. We have to insist that our government change its priorities. We must curtail our insane military spending and stop the flow of drugs into this country. We must mobilize our material and spiritual resources to find quickly a safe, effective cure for A.I.D.S. We must resolve, as a society, to have courage and compassion and to do all in our power to succor its poor victims. The first step is to defend their human rights.

"Systematic testing is nondiscriminatory in the very literal sense that it targets people without regard to their race, gender, color, or sexual preference."

Mandatory AIDS Testing Does Not Violate the Right to Privacy

Gary L. Bauer

Does preventing a possible AIDS epidemic warrant suspending the right to privacy for certain people? Many social commentators believe it does. In the following viewpoint, Gary L. Bauer, the undersecretary for the US Department of Education, writes that mandatory testing is necessary to combat AIDS. Bauer argues that routine testing is needed to protect all American citizens not infected with the AIDS virus. He believes national health concerns take precedence over civil liberties.

As you read, consider the following questions:

1. According to the author, who will eventually pay the costs of AIDS?
2. Why does Bauer advocate mandatory testing over voluntary testing?
3. In the author's opinion, who has a right to know if a person is carrying the AIDS virus?

Gary L. Bauer, "The Case for Routine Testing," *The World & I,* November 1987. Reprinted with the author's permission.

In the face of mounting infection and casualties from the deadly disease AIDS, it is time to stop treating this as a politically protected epidemic. It is imperative that we move forward with the routine health measures that have enabled us to contain epidemics in the past, such as the syphilis epidemic earlier in this century. Routine testing in most cases, and mandatory testing in some, as proposed by President Reagan, is a necessary first step in this process.

Consider the startling facts about the disease. Today there are more than 40,000 AIDS cases and 20,000 deaths. The National Academy of Sciences estimates that between 1 million and 1.5 million Americans are infected with the virus. This may be a conservative estimate.

Even more chilling are the rates at which the disease is spreading. Four years ago there were only 1,500 AIDS cases. A year ago there were about 16,000 cases with 8,100 deaths. The numbers have been virtually doubling every year. If the rates persist, the U.S. Surgeon General calculates that we could have a quarter of a million AIDS cases by 1990.

A Costly Disease

In addition to ravaging lives, AIDS also threatens to ravage the nation's economy. It costs approximately $1,000 a day to treat an AIDS patient in the hospital. As the number of patients increases, who is going to bear the enormous costs, which almost inevitably exceed the victim's ability to pay? Either the government or the insurance industry will be faced with a staggering bill, estimated at $10 billion by 1991. Researchers Anne Scitovsky of the Palo Alto Medical Foundation and Dorothy Rice of the University of California place the total economic cost of AIDS by 1991, including the price of lost productivity, at $65 billion. Ultimately, this cost will be paid by taxpayers and citizens.

How do we begin to approach these daunting facts and probabilities? Three simple criteria should govern all AIDS policy. First, we should do everything we can to find a cure. Second, we should treat with compassion victims who are suffering from the disease. Last, but certainly not least, we should take all necessary measures to protect Americans not infected with AIDS.

There is no question that the government is assiduously backing research efforts to cure AIDS. In addition to private and corporate research under way, this year [1987] the Reagan administration plans to spend more than $300 million on AIDS research. Next year [1988] we will spend $413 million. In an era of budget deficits, there is no stinginess in funding this high-priority project.

The administration is also working to dismantle regulatory barriers so that drugs now confined to the pharmaceutical laboratory can be available in the marketplace. As President Reagan said, "It

153

makes no sense and in fact it is cruel to keep the hope of new drugs from dying patients." The treatment drug AZT has been introduced to the market in record time, circumventing the usual red tape.

In addition to these measures, it is essential that we have a widespread and systematic program of AIDS testing if we are going to protect those Americans who are not yet ill. The reason is fairly obvious. We have to start by knowing all the facts about AIDS. We need to know who the victims of the disease are and how widespread the disease is. We cannot speculate about this; we need sound data.

Whose Rights?

Without massive, mandatory testing, Americans will surely face widespread violations of their rights and liberties.

Testing won't endanger personal freedoms. The danger to freedom is posed by AIDS.

Unless AIDS is stopped soon, we'll face catastrophic medical bills and deaths that are unprecedented. And the high costs and heightened fears could drive us to widespread violations of others' rights.

Lawrence Wade, *Washington Times*, May 28, 1987.

The routine testing that the president supports is not very different from measures taken in the past to deal with threatening epidemics. When the syphilis epidemic broke out in the 1930s, for example, Connecticut was the first state to adopt mandatory premarital blood tests. Other states followed rapidly. According to Allan Brandt, professor of medicine at Harvard, this legislation helped bring about a sharp reduction in the infant mortality rate from syphilis.

Yet many health groups and civil liberties advocates vehemently oppose routine or mandatory AIDS testing. Part of the reason is that they regard AIDS as predominantly an issue of rights instead of an issue of public health. They seem to ignore the fact that during serious health crises, measures must be taken both to treat victims and protect the general population.

Voluntary Testing

Voluntary testing has been proposed as a preferable alternative to systematic or mandatory testing. The reason, advocates say, is that two of the main risk groups, homosexuals and drug users, have historically been victims of public prejudice and will be scared underground by routine testing.

The main problem with voluntary testing is that it subjects the

154

safety of the general population entirely to the discretion of high-risk groups. If high-risk individuals feel like being tested, the rest of us are safer. If they do not, we are not.

It is reasonable to assume, however, that if everyone is being tested, then homosexuals and drug users will feel perfectly natural about stepping forward for testing. By contrast, these high-risk groups may not take the initiative under voluntary testing precisely because it would identify them as likely members of high-risk groups. Heterosexuals could shun testing for fear of being considered members of those groups.

Systematic testing is nondiscriminatory in the very literal sense that it targets people without regard to their race, gender, color or sexual preference. It is an effort to locate the AIDS virus no matter where it exists.

Finally, voluntarism in any policy only makes sense when there is a compelling reason to believe that the individuals who need to be tested will choose on their own to do so. But this is by no means obvious. It is intuitively reasonable that many people who think they might have AIDS might prefer not to know—after all, in the absence of a cure they gain little from knowledge. Indeed, if they find out they do have AIDS, that is information it is not easy to live with.

National Health

Furthermore, the advocates of voluntary testing admit that fear of prejudice or social sanction might keep many members of high-risk groups away from testing sites. If this is so, then overriding social objectives such as national health may mean that we cannot follow a laissez-faire approach when it comes to testing.

It is very important to take note of the voluntary nature of the testing policy for most groups. Routine testing means that individuals can refuse to be tested. Of course, this places the burden of opting out on them. Opting out may carry some social stigma, but this is desirable: The goal is to create incentives for people to be tested and disincentives for them to refuse.

The right to refuse, however, even in the face of the health risks is a clear indication of the importance this country attaches to civil rights and civil liberties. The national health benefit is so important and urgent that we may pressure the individual to conform, through education and through the methodology of routine testing. But we will not sacrifice individual liberties in the process.

One obvious deterrent to people stepping forward to be tested for AIDS is the fear of discriminatory treatment if they test positive. This is a legitimate fear. We must do what we can to allay such fears, both through education of the general public and through reasonable legal protection for victims. We should not, however, convert proper concern for unreasonable mistreatment

Bob Englehart, reprinted with permission.

of AIDS victims into an antidiscrimination mania that puts the general population at risk or forces individuals to endanger themselves.

A Right To Know

To be specific, there is no reason to think that renting a room or apartment to an AIDS victim places the landlord at any risk whatsoever. Similarly, it is clear that most occupations pose no risk of AIDS transmission. I say "most occupations" because there are jobs where there could be a risk. In the health profession, the risk becomes generally greater. Where operations and surgical procedures are involved, there is a good deal of exposure to blood. It is unconscionable to make nurses and doctors place themselves at risk without knowledge that the person they are treating has AIDS. If this is still part of the agenda of gay rights groups or civil liberties groups, they should reconsider it. Reasonable measures to ensure confidentiality within the medical confines can be taken without endangering innocent lives.

There will always be some trade-off between maximizing the protections guaranteed to AIDS victims in order to encourage them to come forward and minimizing the dangers posed to the rest of the population. Here good judgment should prevail in an atmosphere of civility. We have had too much dogmatism from all sides. The presumption should generally favor the person who is not yet infected, simply because his or her life is still intact.

What should be done with information raised through testing? There are some who argue that it should simply be used for statistical purposes. But that is inadequate. Random polling from selected samples could probably provide more useful statistical data. The purpose of testing people is to use that information prudently and selectively to ensure the objectives outlined above.

A health worker has a right to know if a patient is carrying the virus. A woman is entitled to know whether her prospective husband may be carrying the disease because of previous high-risk behavior. Our society has a right to bar entry into the country to those with the virus, just as we do now for other communicable diseases.

The Case for Testing

As treatment drugs become available, the case for testing becomes even stronger. How else will someone know whether they need to begin a particular therapy? Besides, the incentive to come forward and be tested will be greater because people will feel that there is something to be gained even if they do test positive.

We should approach this whole problem with compassion and nuance. We should face the dilemma with courage and determination. We should not let ignorance cloud our thinking. And we should not let special interest groups stand in the way of the health measures that have to be taken.

"The Court has redefined who is entitled to the right of privacy. Married individual have such a right, but homosexual individuals do not."

Anti-Sodomy Laws Violate the Right to Privacy

Jo Marie Escobar

In *Bowers v. Hardwick*, a controversial 1986 case, the US Supreme Court ruled that sodomy is not a protected practice. Therefore, state laws prohibiting sodomy cannot be repealed on constitutional grounds. In the following viewpoint, Jo Marie Escobar argues that the sodomy decision weakened the right to privacy. Escobar, a law student at the Western State University College of Law, criticizes the Supreme Court for its flawed reasoning and discriminatory attitude toward homosexuals in the *Hardwick* case.

As you read, consider the following questions:

1. What examples does the author give of the Supreme Court's "conclusionary thinking"?
2. Why does Escobar criticize the Court's reliance on historical moral standards?
3. Why does the author believe heterosexuals should be concerned about this decision?

Jo Marie Escobar, "*Bowers v. Hardwick*: Redefining the Right to Privacy," *Western State University*, Volume 14:1, 1986. Reprinted with permission.

In *Bowers v. Hardwick* the United States Supreme Court, by a 5-4 majority, upheld the Georgia sodomy statute. In so doing, the High Court has redefined the right to privacy. It certainly now excludes any right to engage in homosexual sodomy, even when the activity is performed in private between two consenting adults. This redefinition appears to greatly narrow the privacy right, casting in doubt the viability of, and possibly threatening rights enunciated in, previous decisions.

The Georgia statute which was challenged by Michael Hardwick criminalizes two different activities: sodomy and aggravated sodomy. Michael Hardwick's case presented a very pure right to privacy issue: whether the due process clause of the fourteenth amendment prohibits state laws which ban consensual sodomy between two adults. The statute is neutral as to the sex of the person who is engaged in the sodomous conduct; it bans "[a] person" from engaging in sodomy. The opinion by Justice White was, therefore, disquietingly incomplete in its reasoned analysis of the question presented by the facts. The majority phrased the issue of the case as "whether the Federal Constitution confers a fundamental right upon homosexuals to engage in sodomy and hence invalidates the laws of the many States that still make such conduct illegal and have done so for a very long time."

The Court's phrasing of the issue determined that it was not about to join the appellee's position. It came as no shock that the Georgia law was held to be valid "as applied" to Michael Hardwick. What was shocking and disturbing was the basis on which the Court found the law to be valid. This Comment will critically analyze the incompleteness of the opinion in *Hardwick*, the conclusionary approach used in lieu of reasoned analysis, the avoidance of the statute itself, and the apparent redefinition of privacy which lurks in *Hardwick*.

History of the Case

The Atlanta Police arrested Michael Hardwick on August 3, 1982, because he had committed the crime of sodomy with a consenting male adult in the bedroom of his own home. Charges were brought, and after the preliminary hearing, Hardwick was bound over to the Superior Court. The District Attorney, however, decided not to present the case to the grand jury unless further evidence developed.

Hardwick, joined by John and Mary Doe, filed suit challenging the constitutionality of the Georgia statute. Hardwick attacked the law as violative of his fundamental right to privacy as a practicing homosexual, under the due process clause of the fourteenth amendment, his right to equal protection under the fourteenth amendment, and his right to freedom of association under the first amendment. The Does challenged the law as violative of their right to marital privacy under the due process clause of the fourteenth amendment. . . .

First year law students are taught the horrors of "conclusionary" thinking and that words such as "evidently" and "obviously" are poor substitutes for reasoning. It is, therefore, terribly disturbing to read Justice White's language in the majority opinion. At critical points Justice White uses such conclusionary words in place of any type of analysis. In the seventh paragraph of the opinion, it is said that "[a]ccepting the decisions in these cases and the above descriptions of them, *we think it evident* that none of the rights announced in those cases bears any resemblance to the claimed constitutional right of homosexuals to engage in acts of sodomy that is asserted in this case." Three paragraphs later, in distinguishing the Court's phrasing of the right at issue in *Hardwick* from formulations of fundamental rights announced in other cases, Justice White again employs non-analysis: "*It is obvious* to us that neither of these formulations would extend a fundamental right to homosexuals to engage in acts of consensual sodomy."

Gay Rights

I am not going to speak in legalese, or cite the wretched decisions of the Supreme Court against us, or quote you lines from the Constitution or its Fourteenth Amendment or from the Bill of Rights. I am only going to say that some 25 million people constitute a sizable minority who are entitled to the same rights as everyone else.

Larry Kramer, *New York Native*, October 12, 1987.

With due respect to the learned Justice, it is not "evident" to many that the rights previously announced bear no resemblance to the right claimed by Hardwick. Most commentators have described the line of cases distinguished by the majority more broadly than does the Court in this case. Other courts have seen the same line of cases cited in *Hardwick* as standing for much more than a right to determine whether to bear or beget a child. To announce that there is no resemblance between Hardwick's asserted right to privacy and that previously described and that this dissimilarity is "obvious," in light of the substantial case law and comment arguing the opposite, is truly unprincipled. The Court, without acknowledging it, has narrowed the right of privacy to its barest minimum, and phrased Hardwick's challenge so as to place it well outside the new narrow reach of the right to privacy. It is then possible for the Court to airily announce that it is "evident" that there is no connection. . . .

The problem with the Court's phrasing of the issue is that the Georgia statute does not ban just homosexual sodomy. A fair reading of the statute "reveals that the majority has distorted the question this case presents." The law prohibits a *person* from engaging in sodomy; the sex of either participant is irrelevant. Heterosexual sodomy, including marital sodomy, is also a crime in Georgia. In fact, most prosecutions under the Georgia law have arisen out of heterosexual situations. In light of the breadth of Georgia's statute, it is hard to understand why the Court chose to focus solely on the appellee's homosexuality. The statute makes clear that the first issue is whether Georgia can prohibit *a person* from engaging in sodomy.

The Court slanted the case to focus only on Hardwick's "as applied" challenge. As such, the only issue was homosexual sodomy, and this "[c]hoice of language to describe a subject can and [did] affect the substantive message." The Court found it quite easy to uphold a law which prohibits homosexual sodomy, as these laws have been around for "a very long time." It is most disturbing to see the Court use tricks of phraseology rather than honest analysis which is demanded by the facts.

The dissenters disagreed that the case was about a fundamental right to engage in homosexual sodomy, rather, it was "about 'the most comprehensive of rights and the right most valued by civilized men,' namely, 'the right to be let alone.'" This does seem a more neutral and accurate description of Hardwick's challenge. Hardwick, who happens to be a homosexual person (an irrelevant fact under the Georgia law) challenged a law which prohibits a person from engaging in consensual sodomy. Differently stated, does a person have a fundamental right to be left alone in his consensual sexual activity? The Court said that if the nature of that activity is sodomy, the answer is no. By extension, any activity which has been anciently proscribed, whether reasonably or not, could be so proscribed today. Proscription without any reason or analysis except "it has always been thus" is blatant discrimination. As the dissent forcefully states, the majority's opinion represents nothing but intolerance of the differences among people. . . .

Erosion of Privacy

The Court solely focused on the adjective with which Hardwick described himself: homosexual. By such a casual analysis, focusing totally on the adjectives used to describe a litigant, the Court has redefined who is entitled to the right of privacy. *Married* individuals have such a right, but *homosexual* individuals do not. Surely the Court cannot allow such an erosion of a precious right to long stand.

In any event, the opinion makes clear that the right to privacy is quite narrow and may now be limited to those associations and behaviors of which the majority approve. Since homosexual sodomy is neither an approved association nor behavior, it is not entitled to protection. "Proscriptions against that conduct have ancient roots. . . . Sodomy was a criminal offense of common law and was forbidden by the laws of the original thirteen states when they ratified the Bill of Rights." The right of homosexual people to engage in sodomy [is] still denied, with no reasons except that such proscriptions are ancient. To substantiate that, the Court relied on the criminal statutes in force in the United States in 1791, 1868, and 1961. The foregoing statutes and one law review article provide the only support for the majority's decision. As Justice Blackmun said,

> It is revolting to have no better reason for a rule of law than that so it was laid down in the time of Henry IV. It is still more revolting if the grounds upon which it was laid down have vanished long since, and the rule simply persists from blind imitation of the past.

The grounds upon which sodomy was proscribed may well have disappeared. Although exact statistics are impossible to obtain, apparently both heterosexual and homosexual persons engage in sodomous behavior as part of their sexual activity. It is unclear whether a majority of the people of the State of Georgia would want sodomy criminalized, or whether that is, in fact, the state interest which would be asserted and proved by the State. There may well be other, and more compelling grounds that the State could show to justify its statute, but it should have been put to its proof by the Court affirming the Court of Appeals and remanding the case for further proceedings. . . .

Sexual Police

The question of whether society accepts the intrusion of police, courts, and legislators in the sphere of sexuality is far from resolved. Because of their intrusive nature, these laws necessitate methods of enforcement that are unwieldy, cumbersome, and unacceptable to a public accustomed to broad sexual privacy. No police department could nor should ever monitor the sexual behavior of citizens. Sodomy laws are clearly unenforceable as they are written but they are routinely used against gay men and lesbians, as well as other vulnerable populations.

Sue Hyde, *Gay Community News*, March 15-21, 1987.

Other privacy cases have protected certain associational interests. These have centered on the family, marriage and procreation, and, by implication, end there. It has seemed reasonable to some that the familial relationships which have been protected are very much like the alternate lifestyle adopted by committed homosexual persons. Professor Kenneth L. Karst once commented that "the freedom of intimate association extends to homosexual associations as it does to heterosexual ones. All the values of intimate association are potentially involved in homosexual relationships; all have been impaired, in various ways, by governmental restrictions on homosexual conduct. . . ." The intimate connection between people, be they heterosexual or homosexual, which culminates in sexual activity is very private and not any concern of government. Such intimacy is a vital and necessary part of adult life. The human being has a crucial psychological need to share sexual love, which requires some form of physical action for its fulfillment and expression.

Those individuals who choose sodomy as a manner of expressing consensual physical love now have a censor in the bedroom. Even authors who are outspoken critics of homosexual behavior decry criminalization of that conduct. [As Aro Karlen said,] "While I favor the repeal of the criminal statutes, this repeal must not happen on the basis that homosexuality is normal, but on the entirely different legal principle that sexual acts taking place in private between consenting adults should be beyond the reach of the law."

The Court had an opportunity to send a message that homosexual persons must be treated equally, but chose instead to treat them as something less than full persons. The Court refused to grant to homosexual individuals the same freedom of association and fundamental right to privacy to which a married person is entitled. This diminishes the individual right to privacy, and raises many questions. Is this the end of an individual right to privacy? Is it the beginning of the end of *Roe v. Wade*, as the philosophical underpinnings have now been laid? If individuals continue to enjoy the right of privacy, which individuals? The Court is obviously concerned with any expansion of those rights "that have little or no textual support in the Constitutional language." Disturbingly, the Court cited all the privacy cases from *Griswold* to *Carey* as examples of such cases. This casts grave doubts on the continued existence of these rights.

Disturbing Questions

The facts of *Hardwick* had caused many writers to hope that this would be the case in which homosexual persons were finally accepted as full citizens. The challenge was quite pure, with no competing interests. Do consenting adults have a right to privacy in their consensual sexual acts?

The Court answered that some individuals do have such a right perhaps, but that some definitely do not. It said so in an opinion which is remarkable for its lack of depth and analysis, and lack of apparent concern for the effect of the holding on either the litigant or the homosexual public generally. While the holding may well frustrate homosexual persons, the absence of analysis of the real issue should make them furious.

For non-homosexuals, the opinion should still leave grave concern. The right to privacy to which they have become accustomed over the past decade or so is under attack. It has been narrowed and redefined to include adjectives to help determine what level of review the Court will use. The rights of unmarried persons appear to be in some jeopardy, and even married persons can take little comfort from *Hardwick*'s refusal to clearly indicate that the Georgia statute would be unconstitutional if applied to them.

Hardwick is a most disturbing opinion which leaves numerous unanswered questions in its wake. The biggest question is whether *Hardwick* is an aberration or whether the Court is beginning a complete redefinition of the right to privacy.

"To hold that the act of homosexual sodomy is somehow protected as a fundamental right would be to cast aside millennia of moral teaching."

Anti-Sodomy Laws Do Not Violate the Right to Privacy

Christopher W. Weller

Christopher W. Weller is a corporate lawyer who was an editor for the *Cumberland Law Review* when he wrote the following viewpoint. In the viewpoint, Weller states that the Supreme Court correctly ruled in *Bowers v. Hardwick* that the Constitution does not protect all sexual activity between consenting adults. He believes that moral laws, such as those prohibiting sodomy, do not violate the right to privacy and are justified because they serve in the state's best interest.

As you read, consider the following questions:

1. According to the author, what are the roots of laws against sodomy?
2. In Weller's opinion, why are homosexual activities not protected by the right to privacy?
3. Why does the author argue that sodomy is not a fundamental right?

Christopher W. Weller, *"Bowers v. Hardwick*: Balancing the Interests of the Moral Order and Individual Liberty," *Cumberland Law Review*, vol. 16, no. 3, 1986. © 1986 by Cumberland Law Review. Used by permission.

During the past several decades, there has been a distinct shift in the law, decreasing the state's paternal role as guardian of its citizens, and defining a less restrictive role emphasizing personal autonomy. Specifically, this trend has manifested itself in the realm of human sexuality as the Supreme Court has continuously redefined the government's regulatory power in this area. Although the Court has established constitutional protection for the heterosexual populace regarding such decisions as procreation and family life, it has just recently addressed definitively the issue of whether the Constitution provides the same protection for homosexuals who engage in consensual sexual acts in the privacy of their homes. For years the courts and legal commentators struggled with this question of personal autonomy. Although some remain eager to expand constitutional protection to the area of consensual homosexual acts, others are more reluctant to provide such protection. The protracted period of confusion and speculation is now over, as the Court has decided the case of *Bowers v. Hardwick*, a Georgia case addressing this issue of homosexual rights. . . .

The Case

In *Hardwick v. Bowers*, the defendant was arrested for engaging in sodomy with a consenting male in the bedroom of his own home in violation of a Georgia statute which criminalized such activity. Hardwick filed suit requesting the federal district court to declare the Georgia sodomy statute unconstitutional. The district court granted the defendants' motion to dismiss, holding that the plaintiff had no legal claim. . . .

On appeal, the Eleventh Circuit, following a lengthy analysis establishing the plaintiff's standing to sue, found that the constitutional right to privacy extended to private, consensual, homosexual acts. Consequently, the court reversed and remanded the case to the district court for further proceedings at which the state would be required to demonstrate a compelling state interest to justify regulation of such activity. . . .

After establishing its right to render a decision on the merits of the case, the court applied a broad interpretation of the privacy doctrine, holding intimate associations were constitutionally protected. Such protection extended to homosexual association, because it resembled the intimate association of marriage. The court found that the activity was "quintessentially private and lies at the heart of an intimate association beyond the proper reach of state regulation.". . .

Law and Morality

Regardless of the philosophical considerations underlying the relationship between law and morality, the established standards for recognizing or denying the existence of individual rights are

the provisions of the Constitution and the Supreme Court's interpretation thereof. Prior to the Court's decision in *Hardwick*, there
were numerous constitutional attacks on sodomy statutes based
on arguments of privacy, vagueness, overbreadth, cruel and
unusual punishment, equal protection, and violations of the
establishment clause. This section will briefly analyze some of
those arguments.

The condemnation of sodomy is rooted in the Judeo-Christian
heritage; both the Old and New Testaments openly condemn such
behavior, as did the writings of early Christian theologians. The
language of many sodomy statutes evidences their religious origin
and nature, particularly those statutes containing the religiously-
based language of Blackstone referring to sodomy as the "crime
against nature."

The religious origins of sodomy statutes have not remained un-
noticed by the homosexual community. Several establishment
clause challenges have been initiated against legislation proscribing sodomy. Mere religious origins, however, are not dispositive
of the constitutional issue. A proper establishment clause challenge
requires some demonstration that the law connotes sponsorship,
financial support, and active involvement of the sovereign in
religious activities. . . .

No Public Protection

As a teacher of morality and a citizen, I want to protect the rights
of all citizens, but I cannot support public protection or sanction-
ing of sexual activity or a way of life which compromises the nor-
mativeness of heterosexual marital intimacy.

Joseph Cardinal Bernardin, *Commonweal*, December 26, 1986.

Prior to the Supreme Court's disposition of *Hardwick*, the most
predominant argument employed by advocates of the expansion
of constitutional protection for individuals who engage in private,
consensual, homosexual acts was the right to privacy. Although
many courts examined the privacy argument, there was no general
agreement in their decisions. The propriety of expansive interpretations was, however, questionable. Indeed, the Supreme Court
decisions addressing the right to privacy did not seem to support
such a broad extension of the doctrine.

Although the concept of an implicit right to privacy has existed
for many years, the Court did not constitutionally recognize individual privacy as a fundamental right until the *Griswold v. Connecticut* decision. In *Griswold*, the Court invalidated a Connecticut
statute prohibiting the use of contraceptives by married persons.
Although some courts have interpreted *Griswold* as establishing

an expansive right to sexual freedom, the privacy issue in that decision inhered in the marital relationship and was limited to the
important familial decision of contraception. Furthermore, in his
concurrence in *Griswold*, Mr. Justice Goldberg, adopting Mr.
Justice Harlan's dissent in *Poe v. Ullman*, explicitly stated:
"Adultery, homosexuality and the like are sexual intimacies which
the State forbids . . . but the intimacy of husband and wife is
necessarily an essential and accepted feature of the institution of
marriage. . . ."

Although some lower courts have held that the privacy doctrine
does include the right to engage in private, consensual, homosexual acts, prior to their disposition of *Hardwick*, the Supreme Court
had never indicated such a broad application of the privacy doctrine would be constitutionally mandated. On the contrary, several
justices expressly recognized that the right to privacy did not en-
compass such activity. In fact, the Court has never expressly
recognized the right of heterosexual couples to engage in sodomy.
The most that can be said is that there was a footnote or two in-
dicating that the issue of private, consensual, sexual relations had
not been exhausted. It seems unrealistic to have believed that the
Court would have relegated such an important decision to a single
ambiguous footnote. . . .

No Fundamental Right

In a narrow 5-4 decision, the Supreme Court upheld the Georgia
sodomy statute and concluded that the Constitution did not confer a fundamental right upon homosexuals to engage in such acts,
however privately practiced. The Court's decision was based on
a four-part rationale.

First, Justice White, writing for the majority, reasoned that "prior
privacy decisions did not support the proposition that any kind
of private sexual conduct between consenting adults [was] constitutionally insulated from state proscription." Rather, previous
decisions defining the zone of privacy limited such protection to
areas involving childrearing, education, family relationships, procreation, marriage, contraception, and abortion. Additionally, the
Court distinguished *Stanley v. Georgia*, holding that the decision
was firmly grounded in the first amendment and did not involve
the privacy doctrine.

Next, the Court emphasized the historical underpinnings of
sodomy laws by tracing their roots back to ancient biblical foun-
dations, through the Middle Ages in England, and through our
nation's historical enactment of the due process clauses of the fifth
and fourteenth amendments. In his concurrence, Chief Justice
Burger echoed the majority opinion, noting that "[t]o hold that
the act of homosexual sodomy is somehow protected as a fundamental right would be to cast aside millennia of moral teaching."
Likewise, Justice Powell stated in his concurrence that he could

not say "that conduct condemned for hundreds of years has now become a fundamental right."

Moreover, Justice White stressed that the Court, in order to avoid illegitimacy, should be very reluctant to expand the substantive reach of the fifth and fourteenth amendments when dealing "with judge-made constitutional law having little or no recognizable roots in the language or design of the Constitution." Applying this restrictive view of the due process clause, the Court held the right to engage in homosexual sodomy failed to qualify as a fundamental right, because it was not "'implicit in the concept of ordered liberty,' such that 'neither liberty nor justice would exist if [they] were sacrificed.'"

The Real Concept of Privacy

The conventional theory regards privacy as a kind of idol. But it is not an idol. Rather it is an essential condition for the full, rich and creative development of human personality. And while the Georgia decision tends to undermine the idolistic notion of privacy, there is no reason that it should injure the more adequate notion.

David R. Carlin Jr., *America*, August 9, 1986.

Finally, the Court . . . held the maintenance of the moral order to be a sufficient rationale to support the constitutionality of the Georgia statute. White noted that "the law . . . is constantly based on notions of morality, and if all laws representing essentially moral choices are to be invalidated under the Due Process [sic] clause, the courts will be very busy indeed." Furthermore, the *Hardwick* majority recognized that the respondent's argument lacked any limiting principle, that "it would be difficult, except by fiat, to limit the claimed right to homosexual conduct while leaving exposed to prosecution adultery, incest, and other sexual crimes even though they are committed in the home.". . .

Conclusion

The Court's decision in *Bowers v. Hardwick* provides the essential guidance which was lacking in this important area of constitutional jurisprudence. Previously, the volatile nature of the issues of privacy rights, homosexuality, and the relationship between law and morals fostered numerous constitutionally bankrupt opinions. The central issue, however, was not really whether private consensual homosexual acts should be proscribed. Rather, it was the transcending question of whether the state has the authority to enact morals legislation considered essential to promote the public welfare. While majoritarian norms alone should never be dispositive of the constitutionality of any statute, as long as no fundamental rights are implicated and the legislation is rationally related to a constitutionally consistent objective, it is not subject to judicial invalidation. As so eloquently stated by the late Justice Hugo Black: "I like my privacy as well as the next one, but I am nevertheless compelled to admit that government has a right to invade it unless prohibited by some specific constitutional provision."

Ranking Right to Privacy Concerns

This activity will allow you to explore the values you consider important in making decisions concerning the right to privacy. A tension exists between the state's duty to preserve the interests of the nation and its obligation to protect the individual's right to privacy. The cartoon below illustrates an example of this tension. The two stage hooks represent the opposing philosophies of individual freedom vs. a need for AIDS testing. Some people advocate widespread testing to discover those who carry the AIDS virus. Others believe that individual freedoms must be preserved even in the face of an epidemic. The cartoonist suggests that this ongoing debate is secondary to the need to get the deadly disease, AIDS, off center stage.

Jerry Barnett. Reprinted with permission, Indianapolis News.

When doing the following exercise, consider when the right to privacy could legitimately be suspended. For example, to safeguard national security all Central Intelligence Agency [CIA] officers periodically take lie detector tests to screen out possible spies. Also consider what reasons would not justify suspension of the right to privacy. For example, merely because a person looks suspicious does not mean the police have a right to search that person's home for evidence of illegal activity.

Step 1. Below is a list of events that involve some aspect of the right to privacy. For each one, indicate whether or not you think it is a justifiable suspension of the right to privacy. *If it is justifiable, put a J beside the event; if not, put an N.*

_____ The owner of a professional football team orders urinalysis tests for all his players because many teams in the league have had drug problems.

_____ The local FBI office orders a wiretap of the phones used by a radical student organization that calls for a violent overthrow of the US government.

_____ A political candidate gives a speech one week before the election detailing her opponent's cheating on a college test twenty years before.

_____ The chief executive officer of a manufacturing company requires a drug test for the leaders of a recent sit-down strike in a plant where no union exists.

_____ A rumor has spread through the US embassy in Czechoslovakia that a staff member has allowed her Czechoslovakian boyfriend into restricted areas of the building. The chief foreign officer orders lie detector tests for all American employees in the embassy to determine if the rumor is true.

_____ The manager of a retail store believes an employee in his department is stealing stereo equipment from the stockroom. He and his assistant manager interview each stockroom employee to discover the possible thief.

_____ A public outcry has arisen over doctors and nurses who carry the AIDS virus but continue to work. To allay public fears, a mandatory AIDS test is done on all health care workers. If tested positive, the workers must quit.

_____ A business magazine publishes a corporate memo intended only for the board of directors detailing their president's poor work performance due to alcoholism.

_____ In an effort to maintain the quality and accuracy of their work, a large defense contractor requires drug tests for assemblers of parts that go into nuclear missiles. If tested positive, the assemblers are fired.

172

_____ The police raid a gay bathhouse and observe several men performing sexual acts. The police arrest the participants and charge them with violating anti-sodomy laws.

_____ Since many other corporate heads are testing for drugs, the owner of a brewery decides to require mandatory urine tests for all her workers.

_____ The central figure in a political scandal has refused media requests for interviews. Political reporters therefore dig through the politician's garbage cans in search of information relating to the case.

_____ The commander of a missile base orders psychological tests for military personnel who would be responsible for launching nuclear weapons.

_____ The driver at fault in a fatal car accident lies in a coma. A judge requests the attending doctors to release information regarding the driver's blood-alcohol content at the time of the crash to determine whether or not criminal charges should be brought.

_____ A television journalist interviews a presidential candidate's high school friends hoping to find disparaging evidence against her.

_____ The opposition party in a European nation prints a photo of the aging prime minister's 23-year-old lover.

_____ A computer firm requires all programmers involved in high-tech research to undergo a nightly body search when leaving work to prevent designs from being sold to competitors.

Step 2. Compare your answers with those of your classmates.

Step 3. Discuss the following questions:
1. What criteria did you use in determining which acts violate the right to privacy and which do not?
2. Do you think a difference exists between a politician's right to privacy and a private citizen's right? If yes, what is the difference?
3. If you were an employer, would your views on the right to privacy differ from those of your employees? Why or why not?

Periodical Bibliography

The following articles have been selected to supplement the diverse views presented in this chapter.

Robert J. Bresler — "Privacy, the Courts, and Social Values," *USA Today*, November 1986.

Joseph Carey — "AIDS: A Time of Testing," *U.S. News & World Report*, April 20, 1987.

David R. Carlin — "Leviathan at Large," *Commonweal*, September 12, 1986.

George J. Church — "Knocking on the Bedroom Door," *Time*, July 14, 1986.

Commonweal — "Testing for AIDS," July 17, 1987.

Harvey V. Fineberg and Mary E. Wilson — "Why Mandatory Testing Is a Bad Idea," *The World & I*, November 1987.

Ira Glasser — "Where the A.C.L.U. Stands on AIDS," *The New York Times*, May 23, 1987.

Ellen Hopkins — "How Often Do You Think About Sex?" *Mademoiselle*, January 1987.

Gary T. Marx — "Drug Foes Aren't High on Civil Liberties," *The New York Times*, February 24, 1986.

Tom Morganthau — "A Question of Privacy," *Newsweek*, September 29, 1986.

Jefferson Morley — "Our Puritan Dilemma," *The New Republic*, December 1, 1986.

The Nation — "The Final Days," July 19-26, 1986.

Anne Marie O'Keefe — "The Case Against Drug Testing," *Psychology Today*, June 1987.

Aric Press — "A Government in the Bedroom," *Newsweek*, July 14, 1986.

Ronald Radosh — "The Right Spirit," *The New Republic*, September 8, 1986.

Charles Rembar — "The A.C.L.U.'s Myopic Stand on AIDS," *The New York Times*, May 15, 1987.

David Robinson Jr. — "Sodomy and the Supreme Court," *Commentary*, October 1986.

Is the Government Responsible for Securing Minority Rights?

CIVIL LIBERTIES

OPPOSING VIEWPOINTS®

Chapter Preface

One hundred years after the signing of the Emancipation Proclamation, the Reverend Martin Luther King Jr. stood in the shadow of the Lincoln Memorial and delivered his famous "I Have a Dream" speech. His speech, presented at the end of the 1963 Freedom March on Washington, signaled the beginning of a new era for the civil rights movement. King said, "There are those of you who are asking the devotees of Civil Rights, 'When will you be satisfied?' . . . [W]e can never be satisfied as long as the Negro's basic mobility is from a smaller ghetto to a larger one. . . . No! No, we are not satisfied, and we will not be satisfied until 'justice rolls down like waters and righteousness like a mighty steam.'" King's assertion emphasizes that the struggle for equal rights is inextricably linked to overcoming the economic realities of racial discrimination and segregation.

The civil rights acts of the 1960s succeeded in eliminating overt segregation, but economic progress has been more difficult to achieve. These acts were supposed to propel blacks and other minorities into the mainsteam of society. After more than two decades, however, US Census Bureau figures indicate that nine million blacks, about one-third of the nation's black population, still suffer from the effects of poverty, unemployment, and racial discrimination. This is roughly three times the poverty rate among whites.

Many civil rights leaders are discouraged by the present situation. As the momentum of the civil rights movement has slowed, its leaders today are sharply divided on how to continue to improve the economic conditions of minorities. Many argue that government has a commitment to provide equal opportunity for minorities. Thus, affirmative action policies must be maintained to ensure economic progress. Opponents, on the other hand, contend that minorities' economic status will improve only as a result of becoming self-reliant, not because of government policies.

The authors of this chapter debate whether or not the government is principally responsible for securing the economic progress as well as the rights of minorities.

"There is no substitute for policies that provide . . . opportunities and create the conditions that make self-help efforts feasible."

Government Policies Will Secure Minority Rights

John E. Jacob

Many black and minority civil rights leaders see the struggle for civil liberties as an effort to eliminate the effects of racial segregation and discrimination. In the following viewpoint, John E. Jacob argues that national policies are needed to provide opportunities for minorities. He is president of the National Urban League, a prominent civil rights organization in the United States.

As you read, consider the following questions:

1. Why is opportunity the key to securing civil rights for minorities, according to Jacob?
2. What examples does Jacob cite to support his argument that government policies can help reduce the effects of racial discrimination?
3. Why does Jacob believe that self-help efforts alone will not improve minority conditions?

John E. Jacob, "The Government and Social Problems," a speech delivered in the Sixth Annual Oliver C. Cox Lecture Series at the John F. Kennedy School of Government, Harvard University on May 1, 1986.

America today is in the midst of a national debate on the proper role of government in dealing with social problems—chief among them the disproportionate poverty and social disorganization afflicting the black community.

During much of the post-war era that debate centered on how our institutional structures could secure civil rights for black citizens and help minorities enter the mainstream of American life.

In recent years, the terms of the debate have changed. Under the leadership of an Administration that labels government itself as "the enemy," the debate centers more and more on how government can effect a strategic withdrawal from social policy. . . .

Government vs. Social Problems

To place the current debate in context, I would like to suggest several propositions:

One—that federal policies have historically promoted economic and social mobility.

Second—that federal policies have led to significant black advances.

Third—that current government policies have intensified the problems facing black and poor people.

American history shows the extent to which government policies shaped opportunities. From the institution of free public education to free land to subsidized railways, Washington's policies always served social ends.

Some of today's critics of social policies were educated under the GI Bill, bought houses with FHA loans, own businesses started with SBA loans, are treated in VA hospitals, drive to work on federally-subsidized highways, educate their children with federally guaranteed loans, and look forward to retirement income from Social Security.

Government bailed out Chrysler. It publicly states that it will not allow large banks to fail. It subsidizes farm interests. Even rugged individualists from the oil patch run to Washington for welfare.

Given that record, the argument that government has no role to play in social policy rings hollow. Government policies created a large middle class and preserved the wealth of the affluent. Government should play an equally decisive role in providing opportunities for the poor.

Civil Rights Means Opportunities

When the federal government did intervene to protect black rights and to reduce poverty, its efforts were by and large successful.

They helped millions out of poverty, secured civil rights for black citizens, and, despite the Reagan counter-revolution, continue to provide opportunities.

Contrary to today's myths, affirmative action and social programs worked.

Affirmative action increased black employment opportunities. A Labor Department study found that federal contractors under affirmative action mandates increased minority employment and promotions at a far higher rate than other employers. . . .

Federal education aid helped raise black children's performance on basic skills tests. Head Start resulted in higher school achievement and better social adjustment. Student aid programs were instrumental in the fivefold increase in black college attendance. . . .

Era of Minority Neglect

The Reagan era has seen a reversal of federal policy—a shift away from intervention to neglect. The result has been to worsen the conditions of poor and black Americans. . . .

The deepest cuts came in programs that invest in education and employment skills, such as job training, which was cut by more than half.

Government Policy: Executive Order 11246

Freedom is not enough. . . . You do not take a person who, for years, has been hobbled by chains and liberate him, bring him up to the starting line of a race and then say, "You are free to compete with all the others," and still justly believe that you have been completely fair. Thus it is not enough just to open the gates of opportunity. All our citizens must have the ability to walk through those gates. . . . To this end equal opportunity is essential, but not enough, not enough.

Lyndon B. Johnson, from a speech delivered at Howard University, 1965.

There is a distinction among welfare programs between universal programs affecting everyone and means-tested programs designed for the poor. Universal programs like social security have not been touched for political reasons. Blacks are less likely to reap the benefits of such programs because they die too young or earn too little to fully share in the payoff.

But blacks typically account for 30 to 40 percent of participants in means-tested programs. And the cuts in those programs reduced the income of poor families by 7.5 percent and drove 2 million people into poverty. . . .

Reality of Race and Poverty

Those who believe that government can and should devise policies that reduce inequality and poverty can point to some considerable past successes.

Those who believe that government cannot and should not implement such policies must defend the results of current policies that have dramatically increased inequality and poverty.

Their only recourse is to say that market forces, unimpeded by government interference, will create wealth and jobs.

That view has only a tenuous relationship to reality. It ignores the persistence of discrimination and its effects. It embodies a fantasy of the blacks and whites lining up at the starting line as equals, when black people run the race of life carrying heavy historical and present burdens on their shoulders.

Everything we know about race and poverty in America suggests that unless the poor are given some extra help—in the form of social policies that enlarge their opportunities—they will not compete on equal terms with the affluent.

The results of the current economic recovery bear that out. We are in the longest sustained economic recovery in memory, and the results are barely perceptible in poverty communities. . . .

Black Unemployment

Black unemployment, which was 6.7 percent in 1970, is stuck at fifteen percent—more than double the white rate. Black unemployment has been in the double digits since the mid-1970s—a . . . Depression with no end in sight.

An April [1987] survey of business leaders found that while they expect the boom to continue, 70 percent predict their employment rolls will either decline or be unchanged this year.

Economic growth alone cannot create sufficient employment opportunities for the poor and the unskilled.

Some argue that even with supportive government policies, many will remain poor because they have neither the skills nor the attitudes to allow them to escape poverty. . . .

The scars borne by those who have been brutalized by poverty and discrimination are deep. But skills can be acquired and attitudes changed.

The primary factor is *opportunity*. People respond to opportunities.

Studies show that children whose parents work do better in school—they see a real-world link between their studies and employment. Dropout rates are lower where students are promised jobs or college admission upon graduation. Other programs demonstrate the eagerness of welfare mothers to obtain skills and jobs.

The Root Cause of Black Poverty

So you can't write off 35 million people who happen to be poor. In all essentials other than income they are not appreciably different from the rest of us.

That is important to remember at a time when the policy debate increasingly centers on the black family.

180

Half of all black families are headed by single women and over two-thirds of poor black children live in those families.

The rise in female-headed households is blamed for the rise in black poverty. It is further asserted that there has been a breakdown in moral values leading to family instability and welfare dependency.

Those assumptions are wrong.

A Long-Term Strategy for Group Advancement

In the long run, the only realistic means to reduce and ultimately eliminate unemployment and poverty in the Black community is a strategy which directly targets the government, not the private sector. Only through massive federal jobs programs, the strict enforcement of affirmative action, housing and human service programs, can the vast majority of Black people actually obtain some measure of economic equality.

Manning Marable, *The Guardian*, January 22, 1986.

The central cause of black poverty and black family instability is the lack of economic opportunity.

The rise in female-headed families is directly linked to the decline in black male employment. . . .

Poverty existed in the past—and as I have pointed out, poverty rates were significantly higher than they were after the Great Society programs.

But America was different then. Most Americans had low and moderate income but there was an abundance of jobs for unskilled laborers. Men might not earn much, but they had jobs, salaries, and self-respect. They were able to assume traditional family roles.

Over the past two decades however, we have seen the systematic destruction of unskilled jobs, including high-paying jobs in auto factories and steel plants.

Economic Oppression of Blacks

Today, blacks are concentrated in industries most affected by job losses and by competition from imports. They live in cities where low-wage manufacturing jobs were replaced by office and skilled service jobs.

Black didn't leave jobs—jobs left blacks.

So the real issue in public policy is not whether federal social programs encourage dependency, but whether they offer opportunities—opportunities to survive the ravages of extreme poverty and opportunities to participate in the economy.

That does not exclude internal community efforts we often call "self-help." Blacks have been picking themselves up by their bootstraps ever since we've been here—even when we didn't have boots.

Today, that tradition continues. In literally hundreds of communities we see creative programs initiated and run by black community-based civil rights agencies and neighborhood groups, ranging from economic development to housing management to food banks.

There is a growing myth today that civil rights organizations are busy fighting yesterday's battles and neglecting today's.

Nothing could be further from the truth. I know of no major civil rights group that says civil rights strategies are the only way to improve the black condition.

But because discrimination remains a stubborn factor in our society, it is a necessary part of our activities. Despite their diversity, civil rights leadership has been consistent in saying that while racism is still a problem, we can't let it become an excuse.

At the same time, those agencies are busy fighting for social policies that would advance the interests of the black poor and of the white poor who vastly outnumber them. . . .

Policies Aid Self-Help Efforts

So blacks do not need any lectures about self-help. We *are* helping ourselves. And it is instructive that the people most deeply involved in those self-help efforts are often the same people who demand more positive national social policies.

Precisely because we are the poorest and most vulnerable part of our society, we know there is no substitute for policies that provide employment and training opportunities and create the conditions that make self-help efforts feasible. We know that *black poverty cannot be significantly altered without changes in social policies.*

Yes, there is much that black people can do—and are doing—for themselves, but the place of blacks in our society will ultimately be determined by national policies that provide opportunities and make full use of all of America's human resources.

I believe that such policies will eventually be adopted because they are in the national interest.

Changing demographics mean that a third of new entrants into the labor force are non-white. A severe labor shortage is predicted before the end of the century.

Unless we equip our neglected minorities with the education and the skills to fully participate in a post-industrial economy, America can expect second-class economic status, a weakened world position, and deep unrest at home.

Rather than commit suicide for the sake of antigovernment ideology, I believe America will return to a more activist social policy.

"There is no substitute for what is to be won through the unaided accomplishments of individual persons."

Government Policies Will Not Secure Minority Rights

Glenn C. Loury

Glenn C. Loury is one of several black intellectuals who believes the focus of the current civil rights movement is wrong. In the following viewpoint, Loury argues that minorities must emphasize individual achievement. Government policies which give blacks preferential treatment undermine civil rights, he contends, because they do not reward individual merit. Loury is a professor of political economy at Harvard's John F. Kennedy School of Government.

As you read, consider the following questions:

1. In Loury's opinion, why does racially preferential treatment destroy the good that it was intended to accomplish?
2. Why, according to Loury, will some forms of racial discrimination not be affected by civil rights policies?
3. What benefits does Loury see for blacks who succeed without help from the white majority?

Glenn C. Loury, "Beyond Civil Rights," *The New Republic*, October 7, 1985. Reprinted by permission of THE NEW REPUBLIC, © 1985, The New Republic, Inc.

There is today a great deal of serious discussion among black Americans concerning the problems confronting them. Many, if not most, people now concede that not all problems of blacks are due to discrimination, and that they cannot be remedied through civil rights strategies or racial politics. I would go even further: using civil rights strategies to address problems to which they are ill-suited thwarts more direct and effective action. Indeed, the broad application of these strategies to every case of differential achievement between blacks and whites threatens to make it impossible for blacks to achieve full equality in American society.

The civil rights approach has two essential aspects: first, the cause of a particular socioeconomic disparity is identified as racial discrimination; and second, advocates seek such remedies for the disparity as the courts and administrative agencies provide under the law.

Civil Rights Strategies Have Limitations

There are fundamental limitations on this approach deriving from our liberal political heritage. What can this strategy do about those important contractual relationships that profoundly affect one's social and economic status but in which racial discrimination is routinely practiced? Choice of marital partner is an obvious example. People discriminate here by race with a vengeance. A black woman does not have an opportunity equal to that of a white woman to become the wife of a given white man. Since white men are on the whole better off financially than black men, this racial inequality of opportunity has substantial monetary costs to black women. Yet surely it is to be hoped that the choice of husband or wife will always be beyond the reach of the law. . . .

The nondiscrimination mandate has not been allowed to interfere much with personal, private, and intimately social intercourse. Yet such exclusive social connections along group lines have important economic consequences. An extensive literature in economics and sociology documents the crucial importance of family and community background in determining a child's later success in life. Lacking the right "networks," blacks with the same innate abilities as whites wind up less successful. And the elimination of racial discrimination in the economic sphere—but not in patterns of social attachment—will probably not be enough to make up the difference. There are thus elemental limits on what one can hope to achieve through the application of civil rights strategies to what must of necessity be a restricted domain of personal interactions.

Social Problem *Within* Black Communities

The civil rights strategy has generally been restricted to the domain of impersonal, public, and economic transactions such as jobs, credit, and housing. Even in these areas, the efficacy of this strategy can be questioned. The lagging economic condition of blacks is due in significant part to the nature of social life *within* poor black communities. After two decades of civil rights efforts, more than three-fourths of children in some inner-city ghettos are born out of wedlock; black high school dropout rates hover near 50 percent in Chicago and Detroit; two-fifths of murder victims in the country are blacks killed by other blacks; fewer black women graduate from college than give birth while in high school; more than two in five black children are dependent on public assistance. White America's lack of respect for blacks' civil rights cannot be blamed for all these sorry facts. This is not to deny that, in some basic sense, most of these difficulties are related to our history of racial oppression, but only to say that these problems have taken on a life of their own, and cannot be effectively reversed by civil rights policies.

Government Can't Develop Individual Responsibility

I thought my grandparents were too rigid and their expectations were too high. . . . But one of their often-stated goals was to raise us so that we could "do for ourselves," so that we could stand on our "own two feet." . . . The most compassionate thing they did for us was to teach us to fend for ourselves and to do that in an openly hostile environment. . . . I was raised to survive under the totalitarianism of segregation, not only without the active assistance of government but with its active opposition. We were raised to survive in spite of the dark oppressive cloud of governmentally sanctioned bigotry. Self-sufficiency and spiritual and emotional security were our tools to carve out and secure freedom. Those who attempt to capture the daily counseling, oversight, common sense, and vision of my grandparents in a governmental program are engaging in sheer folly. Government cannot develop individual responsibility, but it certainly can refrain from preventing or hindering the development of this responsibility.

Clarence Thomas, speech delivered at The Heritage Foundation, June 18, 1987.

Higher education is a case in point. In the not too distant past, blacks, Asians, and women faced severe obstacles to attending or teaching at American colleges and universities, especially at the most prestigious institutions. . . .

Today opportunities for advanced education and academic careers for blacks abound. Major universities throughout the country are constantly searching for qualified black candidates to hire as professors, or to admit to study. Most state colleges and universites near black population centers have made a concerted effort to reach those in the inner city. Almost all institutions of higher learning admit blacks with lower grades or test scores than white students. . . .

Yet, with all these opportunities (and despite improvement in some areas), the number of blacks advancing in the academic world is distressingly low. The percentage of college students who are black, after rising throughout the 1970s, has actually begun to decline. . . .

Meanwhile, other groups traditionally excluded are making impressive gains. Asian-Americans, though less than two percent of the population, make up 6.6 percent of U.S. scientists with doctorates; they constitute 7.5 percent of the students at Yale, and nine percent at Stanford. . . .

Such substantial differences in educational results are clearly a matter of great concern. Arguably, the government should be actively seeking to attenuate them. But it seems equally clear that this is not a civil rights matter that can be reversed by seeking out and changing someone's discriminatory behavior. Moreover, it is possible that great harm will be done if the problem is defined and pursued in those terms.

Creating Academic Difficulties

Take the controversy over racial quotas at the Boston Latin School, the pride and joy of the city's public school system. It was founded before Harvard, in 1635, and it has been recognized ever since as a center of academic excellence. Boston Latin maintains its very high standards through a grueling program of study. . . .

The institution admits its students on the basis of their marks in primary school and performance on the Secondary School Admissions Test. In 1974, when Boston's public schools became subject to court-ordered desegregation, Judge Arthur Garrity considered closing Boston Latin, because the student population at the time was more than 90 percent white. In the end, a racial admissions quota was employed, requiring that 35 percent of the entering classes be black and Hispanic. . . .

Historically the school has maintained standards through a policy of academic "survival of the fittest." . . . Thus, there has always been a high rate of attrition; it is now in the range of 30 percent to 40 percent. But today, unlike the pre-desegregation era, most of those who do not succeed at Boston Latin are minority students. . . . Some advocates of minority student interests have complained of discrimination, saying in effect that the school is not doing enough to assist those in academic difficulty. Yet surely one reason for the poor performance of the black and Hispanic students is Judge Garrity's admissions quota. To be considered for admission, whites must score at the 70th percentile or higher on the admissions exam, while blacks and Hispanics need only score above the 50th percentile.

Thomas Atkins, former general counsel of the NAACP, who has been representing the black plaintiffs in the Boston school desegregation lawsuit, which has been going on for [over] ten years, proposed that the quota at Boston Latin be raised to roughly 50 percent black, 20 percent Hispanics and Asian, and 30 percent white—a reflection of the racial composition of the rest of Boston's public schools. . . . The likely consequence would be that more than three-fourths of those leaving Boston Latin without a degree would be blacks and Hispanics. It is also plausible to infer that such an action would profoundly alter, if not destroy, the academic climate in the school.

Get Government Out of the Way

Civil rights is no longer the big problem for blacks. How are civil right laws going to help thousands of blacks, with diploma in hand, who are semi-literate and (if I can coin a word) ilnumerate? Most blacks who graduate from college score 200 points below the norm on the Graduate Record Examination (GRE) and flunk *en masse* civil service tests. How's civil rights enforcement going to help them? To interpret results such as these as a civil rights issue is counterproductive. . . .

The bottom line is that . . . blacks cannot depend on the politics of government quick fixes. Black people can't afford to wait for government to bring law and order to our neighborhoods and schools. We must do it ourselves.

Walter E. Williams, *Conservative Chronicle*, February 19, 1986.

This is not simply an inappropriate use of civil rights methods, through it is surely that. It is an almost wanton moral surrender. By what logic of pedagogy can these students' difficulties be attributed to racism, in view of the fact that the school system has been run by court order for over a decade? . . . Is there so little faith in the aptitude of the minority young people that the highest standards should not be held out for them? It would seem that the real problem here—a dearth of academically outstanding black high school students in Boston—is not amenable to rectification by court order. . . .

Subtle Danger to Blacks

The danger to blacks of too broad a reliance on civil rights strategies can be subtle. It has become quite clear that affirmative action creates uncertain perceptions about the qualifications of those minorities who benefit from it. In an employment situation, for example, if it is known that different selection criteria are used for different races, and that the quality of performance on the job depends on how one did on the criteria of selection, then in the absence of other information, it is rational to expect lower performance from persons of the race that was preferentially favored in selection. . . .

The broad use of race preference to treat all instances of "underrepresentation" also introduces uncertainty among the beneficiaries themselves. It undermines the ability of people confidently to assert, if only to themselves, that they are as good as their achievements would seem to suggest. It therefore undermines the extent to which the personal success of any one black can become the basis of guiding the behavior of other blacks. Fewer individuals in a group subject to such preferences return to their communities of origin to say, "I made it on my own, through hard work, self-application, and native ability, and so can you!" Moreover, it puts even the "best and brightest" of the favored group in the position of being supplicants of benevolent whites.

And this is not the end of the story. In order to defend such programs in the political arena—especially at the elite institutions—it becomes necessary to argue that almost no blacks could reach these heights without special favors. When there is internal disagreement among black intellectuals, for example, about the merits of affirmative action, critics of the policy are often attacked as being disingenuous, since (it is said) they clearly owe their own prominence to the very policy they criticize. The specific circumstances of the individual do not matter in this, for it is presumed that *all* blacks, whether directly or indirectly, are indebted to civil rights activity for their achievements. The consequence is a kind of "socialization" of the individual's success. The individual's effort to claim achievement for himself (and thus to secure the autonomy and legitimacy needed to deviate from group consensus, should that seem appropriate) is perceived as a kind of betrayal. There is nothing wrong, of course, with acknowledging the debt all blacks owe to those who fought and beat Jim Crow. There is everything wrong with a group's most accomplished persons feeling that the celebration of their personal attainments represents betrayal of their fellows. . . .

Lack of Honor

This problem, in my judgment, remains with us. Its eventual resolution is made less likely by blacks' broad, permanent reliance on racial preferences as remedies for academic or occupational under-performance. A central theme in Afro-American political and intellectual history is the demand for respect—the struggle to gain inclusion within the civic community, to become coequal participants in the national enterprise. This is, of course, a problem that all immigrant groups also faced, and that most have overcome. But here, unlike some other areas of social life, it seems that the black population's slave origins, subsequent racist exclusion, and continued dependence on special favors from the majority uniquely exacerbates the problem.

White Government Can't Help Black America

It is now or never. This is Black America's last chance. Black America must get moving. It must recognize the problem. It must recognize that *it* is the problem. It must recognize that white government cannot help it and probably, to an increasing degree in the future, will not help it. Black America must help itself. It must try to rebuild self-respect—and that means, of course, self-reliance.

Nathaniel O. Stevens, *Lincoln Review*, Fall 1986.

Blacks continue to seek the respect of their fellow Americans. And yet it becomes increasingly clear that, to do so, black Americans cannot substitute judicial and legislative decree for what is to be won through the outstanding achievements of individual black persons. That is, neither the pity, nor the guilt, nor the coerced acquiescence in one's demands—all of which have been amply available to blacks over the last two decades—is sufficient. *For what ultimately is being sought is the freely conveyed respect of one's peers.* Assigning prestigious positions so as to secure a proper racial balance—this as a permanent, broadly practiced policy—seems fundamentally inconsistent with the attainment of this goal. It is a truth worth noting that not everything of value can be redistributed.

Public Policy Won't Bring Equality

If in the psychological calculus by which people determine their satisfaction such status considerations of honor, dignity, and respect are important, then this observation places basic limits on the extent to which public policy can bring about genuine equality. This is especially so with respect to the policy of racially preferential treatment, because its use to "equalize" can actually destroy the good that is being sought on behalf of those initially unequal. It would seem that, where the high regard of others is being sought, there is no substitute for what is to be won through the unaided accomplishments of individual persons.

"Blacks were only due the granting of equal status, equal protection."

Government Should Guarantee Minorities Equality of Opportunity

Clarence M. Pendleton Jr.

Clarence M. Pendleton Jr. is the chairman of the US Commission on Civil Rights. Appointed by President Reagan in 1983, Pendleton advocates eliminating affirmative action, calling the program an idea that was "wrong in the first place." In the following viewpoint, he argues that the Civil Rights Act of 1964 already guarantees that all people should be treated as equals before the law. Pendleton believes that special protections for blacks are actually barriers to opportunity and should be eliminated.

As you read, consider the following questions:

1. How does Pendleton argue that the Constitution recognizes the rights of individuals rather than the rights of groups?
2. Why, according to the author, do many blacks believe that they are due a special preference from the government?
3. Why does Pendleton believe that special protections for blacks are barriers to opportunity?

Clarence M. Pendleton Jr., "Equality of Opportunity, or Equality of Results," *Human Rights*, Fall 1985. Reprinted with permission.

It has been more than 20 years since the Civil Rights Act of 1964 was passed, and the debate over what Congress intended still rages.

During the years, the question has remained: Was the intent of Congress to provide equality of opportunity or equality of results?

For 84 days, the longest debate in its history, the Senate tried to resolve the issue in 1964. We still have not answered the question.

Opportunity vs. Results

Many leading civil rights organizations at that time, led by Senator Hubert Humphrey, argued the equality of opportunity side. Humphrey assured his colleagues time and again that group preferences were not to be tolerated.

There is nothing in Title VII of the bill, he insisted, "that will give any power to the [Equal Employment Opportunity] Commission or to any court to require hiring, firing or promotion of employees in order to meet a racial 'quota' or to achieve a certain racial balance. That bugaboo has been brought up a dozen times; but it is nonexistent."

The opposition believed that, despite the intent of the bill, the effect would be to insure equality of results, as interpreted by the enforcing agencies of government.

The act was passed to substantiate the rights of blacks. However, the bill's language insisted that race, color, religion, and national origin were to limit no one's rights.

Citizens, Individuals, and Persons

The act followed the language and spirit of the 13th, 14th, and 15th amendments to the Constitution. It spoke of "citizens, individuals, and persons," not blacks, not Hispanics, native Americans, Asians, or any other group that might be subject to discrimination.

It seemed as though Justice John Marshall Harlan's famous dissent in *Plessy* v. *Ferguson* would be the law at last: "In view of the Constitution, in the eye of the law, there is in this country no superior, dominant ruling class of citizens. There is no caste here. Our Constitution is color-blind, and neither knows nor tolerates classes among its citizens.

"In respect of civil rights, all citizens are equal before the law. The humblest is the peer of the most powerful. The law regards man as man, and takes no account of his surroundings or of his color when his civil rights as guaranteed by the supreme law of the Land are involved."

Americans thought the eloquent words spoken by Dr. Martin Luther King Jr. from the steps of the Lincoln Memorial were cast in stone. All people, he said, were "to be judged by the content of their character not by the color of their skin."

One would be sadly and grossly mistaken to believe that a color-blind society has been obtained. The implimentation and enforcement of this law, as columnist George Will once described, succeeded in dividing "the majestic national river into little racial and ethnic creeks."

The United States, Will wrote, became "less a nation than an angry menagerie of factions scrambling for preference."

The Breakdown of Civil Rights

The massive societal consensus that demanded passage of the Civil Rights Act of 1964 began to break down in the 1970s. New legislation and an executive order required increased attention to race and ethnicity in hiring by any private or public employer that received federal aid or was subject to government regulation.

It was now required to count how many minorities were recruited, interviewed, trained, hired, admitted, served or enrolled.

Twenty years later, it is still necessary "to count noses" to determine if there is discrimination.

Minorities Need an Economic Liberty Civil Rights Act

Two hundred years after adoption of our Constitution and a quarter century after civil rights activists marched on Washington to remind Americans of the individual rights enshrined in that document, someone ought to be standing up for these fundamental liberties. . . .

The increased welfare spending, quotas, and set-asides that have dominated civil rights policy for the past 25 years have not changed the course of dependency and despair. Even stalwart defenders of this agenda are coming reluctantly to recognize this. So it is an opportune moment to refashion the terms of the civil rights debate—from collectivism to individualism, from coercion to opportunity, from dependency to dignity.

Legislation—filling the void left by the Civil Rights Act of 1964—is one way to start on an alternative agenda. An Economic Liberty Civil Rights Act, guaranteeing the right of every individual to pursue work and business opportunities free from arbitrary governmental constraints, could provide a focal point for a forward-looking civil rights program.

Clint Bolick, *Reason*, November 1987.

That equality of opportunity so ardently fought for and won in 1964 has given way to equality of results through such bureaucratic devices as fair share, proportional representation, special preferences, quotas, goals, timetables, and set-asides.

Today, many blacks believe that the laws were passed to ensure only their civil rights, and that blacks are due a special preference from the government to make up for the despicable institution of slavery. They sincerely believe that the government has not yet made up for past atrocities.

This is where I part company with some of my people. I believe that blacks were only due the granting of equal status, equal protection. I also believe that many of the laws and court decisions that occurred since 1964 were necessary to reassert the constitutional guarantees expressed by the 13th, 14th, and 15th amendments.

Insistence on group preference is a role reversal. Those who marched, struggled and died for equality now want separation.

Enforcement Harms Blacks

In enforcing the Civil Rights Act, the government perpetuated and worsened the situation with a myriad of artificial allotments, considered incentives to assist and propel minorities into America's mainstream.

Those artificial allotments included goals, timetables, quotas and other numerical devices imposed by government to suit its notion of how society should be organized—a society where a person's standing is determined by pigment, ethnicity or gender.

Allocating social benefits on the basis of race or gender has led to bitterness and disharmony. Economist Thomas Sowell expressed a cause for concern when he stated, "There is much reason to fear the harm that [a racial preference] is doing to its supposed beneficiaries, and still more reason to fear the long-run consequences of polarizing the nation. Resentments do not accumulate indefinitely without consequences."

The U.S. Commission on Civil Rights is studying the long- and short-term consequences of these artificial allotments. Some of the issues under study are:

• *Incomes of Americans: ethnic, racial and sex differences.* The commission is examining how employment discrimination, schooling and work experiences have affected income differences between men, women, racial and ethnic groups since the 1940s.

• *Affirmative action in higher education.* Techniques used by universities to increase minority and female representation among students and faculty members will be studied, along with success rates. The study will also assess the effect of affirmative action on different types of institutions and their student bodies, faculties, curricula, standards of admission, grading, progress, and graduation.

• *Voluntary and involuntary methods of achieving school desegregation.* We are studying how busing, magnet schools, open enrollment, and special attendance schools have worked to achieve integration in up to 40 sites. We want to know how long integration was achieved and its effects on the communities involved.

• *State and local civil rights enforcement.* The commission is evaluating how well state and local vocational rehabilitation agencies are enforcing civil rights.

• *Redistricting and minorities.* The commission has started a study of redistricting by state and local governments in order to comply with the one-person, one-vote principle for apportioning representation following 1980 census data.

Protect the Right to Opportunity

I don't think that government should be in the business of parceling out rights or benefits. Rights emanate from the Constitution and from the Declaration. They are there, and they should be protected. I am not confident that Washington is any more moral or stronger than anyone else to assign rights, or even better able to do it. We should be careful not to concede the rights of individuals in our society in order to gain something such as parity. Ultimately that will do us a disservice.

The Equal Employment Opportunity Commission is mandated to protect people's individual rights to equal opportunity. . . .

It is protecting one's right to be free from discrimination; it is not creating or parceling out that right. That right comes through the Constitution and is implemented by Title VII. If the government has any role in this matter, it is the protection of the rights of its citizens from foreign and domestic enemies.

Clarence Thomas, *The Center Magazine,* November/December 1987.

We want to know whether redistricting plans dilute the voting strength of minorities in violation of the Voting Rights Act and the Constitution. We are also examining the effects of various districting plans on the opportunity of minorities to effectively participate in the political process. . . .

The Moral and Constitutional Objective

It is equality of opportunity that allows one to advance toward that laudable goal of a color-blind, race and gender neutral society. Only equality of opportunity will facilitate each individual or group to achieve to the limit of their creativity, imagination and enthusiasm.

Congress and the courts should make a commitment to pursue the moral and constitutional high ground and reject any notion that discrimination can be eliminated or minimized by racial balancing in the form of proportional representation. Nor should Congress condone equality of results in the form of preferential treatment such as quotas, goals, timetables or set-asides.

The main objective of the federal, state and local government must be to provide equal opportunity based upon individual merit. Each of us has an obligation to make sure that our children can compete based upon merit. This means they must be prepared.

A quality education must be available to all children. This nation cannot afford another generation of illiterates of any color.

Desegregation Is Dangerous

Derrick Bell, dean of the University of Oregon Law School and a leading force in early court cases to end segregation, has concluded that while "there is potential strength in the argument that school desegregation is needed to improve society, the danger is that this societal personification of the benefit reduces the priority for correction of the harm suffered directly by blacks to a secondary importance when it should be the primary concern."

As W.E.B. DuBois said years ago, "The black child needs neither segregated schools nor mixed schools. What he needs is an education."

I myself survived and prospered without the so-called benefits of affirmative action and integration. The reason for my survival and success is preparation. I attended the all-black Dunbar High School in Washington, D.C. and was given a special gift.

Those black teachers demanded excellence and I left prepared to go forward. I obtained both post secondary degrees from a black college, Howard University, which gave me the tools necessary to achieve success.

Black Self-Help

We must encourage black people to support black institutions: the black church, black colleges, banks, fraternities, service organizations and countless others. We cannot depend upon philanthrophy and charity to save our institutions.

We must create innovative and effective public policy that opens doors and keeps them open. We should be advocating the relaxation and repeal of various regulations that restrict entry and access to the marketplace.

Not only black Americans would benefit from such advocacy. Is it necessary for a barber or beautician to know the name of every bone in the hand to adequately cut hair? Why should a New York City taxi medallion cost $85,000 when a license in Washington, D.C. is only $200? Licensing only serves to restrict access to the market. How many people have $85,000?

Minimum wage also restricts entry into the market by black teenagers. Even the black mayors in the United States believe this to be true, yet many of us continue to work against initiation of legislation to reduce minimum wage.

Finally, affirmative action must be re-evaluated. A program which began with the best intentions and highest ideals has ended up setting white against black. It has created new protected classes, made victim status desirable and forced society to question the accomplishments of its children.

Most tragically, it has created a generation which sees no need to take risks and will never see its rewards. No quota will make any of us successful. No program of quotas will prevent the last of us from failing. Risk taking should be the engine that propels us to success.

Remove Barriers to Opportunity

Solving the problem of discrimination with more laws and regulations is not the answer. We have a moral responsibility to remove the barriers that deny people access to equal opportunity. We should get rid of special protections that can place more barriers to opportunity.

A passage in *The Essential Rousseau*, "Discourse on Inequality Among Men," written in 1755, sums up the situation:

"Peoples once accustomed to masters are no longer in condition to do without them. If they try to shake off the yoke, they move still farther away from freedom because they confuse it with an unbridled license that is opposed to it, and their revolutions nearly always deliver them into the hands of seducers who only make their chains heavier than before."

"Black gains are eroding and the gap between the races is widening dangerously."

Government Should Guarantee Minorities Equality of Results

Vernon E. Jordan Jr.

Vernon E. Jordan is a distinguished civil rights lawyer. As president of the National Urban League from 1972-1981, he was able to closely monitor the progress of civil rights legislation and the condition of blacks in this country. In the following viewpoint, Jordan argues that the plight of blacks in the South did indeed improve during the 1960s and 70s as a result of civil rights legislation. However, he points out, blacks are still economically disadvantaged. Jordan believes that until the goal of economic equality is finally reached, government leaders must support the enforcement of civil rights laws that ensure black economic progress.

As you read, consider the following questions:

1. According to Jordan, how does the inadequate enforcement of civil rights laws threaten to resegregate the nation?
2. According to the author, why do minorities continue to need preferential treatment in the workforce?
3. Why does Jordan believe that southern political leadership can lead the nation toward becoming a color-blind society?

Vernon E. Jordan Jr., "Let Us Finish the Task," a speech delivered to the Lawyers Club of Atlanta on March 19, 1986.

The South once clung to segregation with a fervor hard to imagine these days. The cry was: "No, not one!", and George Wallace barred the schoolhouse door.

Today the South is the least segregated part of the country east of the Rockies, and George Wallace is elected with the help of black people, whom he once tried to keep from exercising their right to vote. The South has changed, and by changing, it can light a beacon for the rest of the nation. It has experienced the worst of racism and today is experiencing the promise of integration.

But perhaps the greatest danger our region faces is the danger of complacency, the idea that because we've come so far so soon, we have reached our goal. But if the goal is a truly multiracial South in which each and every one of us can develop his or her potential to the fullest, we have a long way to go.

Civil Rights Momentum

I believe southerners should be asking themselves whether the South has changed enough, and whether that change is in the process of being arrested as part of the national withdrawal from efforts to make our society more equal and more just. The challenge today is to make the South the engine of racial progress that helps bring the rest of the country into the twenty-first century.

The South has changed politically. The Voting Rights Act of 1965 and the civil rights law made it possible for the two-party system to come to the region, for a southerner to be elected President of the United States, and for the South to participate in the mainstream of the national economy.

But in racial terms, the South has not changed enough in the economic sphere. The challenge of our times, for the region and for the nation, is to achieve the economic empowerment of black Americans. Unless the racial gap is closed in the economic sphere, there is a danger that the racial politics of the past will continue far into the future, with racially based class divisions becoming the determining factor in the region's socio-political makeup.

Growing National Threat

That danger is national, as well. For black disadvantage is national in scope, and represents the nation's major domestic problem. Widespread poverty and unemployment damage our economy, prevent full use of our productive resources at a time of global economic competition, and threaten a democracy that is based on the full consent and participation of the governed.

Unfortunately, there is a growing feeling, spurred by the Reagan Administration, that race is no longer a significant factor in American life. The Attorney General has campaigned long and hard for the view that we are a color-blind, racially neutral society. His Justice Department has expanded time and energy better used to enforce the civil rights laws, papering the federal courts with briefs arguing against affirmative action and other civil rights measures. The administration has spent months in internal debate over issuing an executive order that would revoke present orders mandating affirmative action for federal contractors. And the Equal Employment Opportunity Commission has changed its guidelines relating to hiring goals and timetables.

The Supreme Court has considered several affirmative action cases and has several more on [its] calendar. Its decision in the *Stotts* case, in 1984, affirming the precedence of seniority agreements over affirmative action in layoffs, triggered a wave of misinterpretations by federal lawyers. The Justice Department's attempt to broaden the ruling far beyond the obvious limits of the case has given new heart to those who would dismantle affirmative action programs.

Racial Facts of Life

Our America will not be restored to greatness unless it comes to grips with the racial facts of life; unless it comes to understand that being poor is different from being rich; that equal opportunity can only come from extending a hand that helps people overcome the disadvantages of race and class. . . .

And making it on your own means the operation of laws and customs to level the track to give everyone an equal chance. It means economic policies that provide jobs of all kinds in a growing economy. It means affirmative action that overcomes the barriers of poverty and discrimination. It means that government removes the factors that victimize and brutalize whole segments of society. It means that the groups shoved to the margin of our society are finally brought into the mainstream through conscious, deliberate policies to overcome their disadvantages.

Calling anything else "equal opportunity" amounts to mislabeled packaging. Worse, it leads to perpetuation of an America divided between white and black, rich and poor, suburban and urban, employed and unemployed.

John E. Jacob, speech delivered at the Annual Conference of the National Urban League, Inc., Atlanta, GA, March 3, 1983.

One of the cases before the Court, involving New York City's sheetmetal union, seeks to overturn a federal court order requiring the union to comply with an affirmative action plan. The Justice Department, which is supporting the union, admits that the union has "an ample record of inexcusable disobedience." But it would allow that disobedience to stand.

That typifies the administration's approach. It agrees that blacks were persistently denied their civil rights, that constitutional rights were violated, and that race was the grounds for exclusion. But at the same time it resists racially based remedies that the courts have consistently ruled were constitutional and that offer the only means of reversing admittedly unconstitutional practices.

Reversing Unconstitutional Practices

It should listen to Justice Blackmun, who wrote in the *Bakke* case:

> In order to get beyond racism we must first take account of race. There is no other way. And in order to treat some persons equally, we must treat them differently.

That seems to me to be self-evident. We cannot erase the burden of past and present discrimination without a temporary period of affirmative action to open opportunities for those denied them for so long.

Even as the administration attempts to stigmatize affirmative action with the label of "reverse discrimination," affirmative action enjoys the support of the business community. Business sees affirmative action as a common sense way to solve the problem of underrepresentation of minorities and women. As the National Association of Manufacturers told a congressional committee last summer:

> Industry does not believe that numerical goals for minority inclusion in the workforce, by themselves, constitute quotas. Business, particularly big business, sets goals and timetables for every aspect of its operation. . . . Setting goals and timetables for minority and female participation is a way of measuring prog- ress and focusing on potential discrimination.

At a time when black gains are eroding and the gap between the races is widening dangerously, affirmative action is more important than ever before. We are *not* a color-blind society. We are *not* a racially neutral society. We are still a society in which race counts; a society in which blackness is a badge of inequality. Lyndon Johnson said it well:

> To be black in a white society is not to stand on level and equal ground. While the races may stand side by side, whites stand on history's mountain and blacks stand in history's hollow. Until we overcome unequal history, we cannot overcome unequal opportunity.

The South knows a lot about overcoming unequal history. As a region, it has been the poor sister of the rest of the nation. Politically, it has been relegated to the margins of the national polity.

Thanks to the destruction of Jim Crow, to the civil rights laws, and to the achievement of a more democratic political life in the region, the South now has a greater influence in the political life of the nation. . . .

American politics today are dangerously close to being a regional politics, with the Democrats strong in the Northeast and the industrial Midwest and the Republicans representing the West and the white South.

Our politics are also more blatantly class-based than in the past. President Reagan's 1984 sweep can be compared to Eisenhower's 1956 victory. Both got 75 percent of the vote of the richest ten percent. But the resemblance ends there. Ike won 56 percent of the working and lower middle class vote—Reagan only 43 percent. Ike even won the vote of the poorest ten percent, getting 59 percent of their ballots. Reagan got less than a third.

Bob Englehart, reprinted with permission.

Republicans will not hold on to the White House in the post-Reagan era unless they can cut across class lines and make inroads in the black vote. Without the President's personality to attract voters otherwise opposed to his policies, the party will have to broaden its base. And it must do so on issues, not on personality, because the post-Reagan Republicans don't have anyone with the President's charm and mass appeal. . . .

The Democrats have the potential to construct a viable coalition that is far broader-based than the narrow Republican coalition that has been in power. Whether they have the wisdom to do it is another question.

I am hopeful they will because it holds the potential of bringing more rational policies to the national scene, and because it can be the seal on the South's emergence to national leadership and political maturity. Above all, the inclusion of southern leadership in a national coalition devoted to restoring the values of justice and fairness in our national life will help the South and the nation complete the job it started some two decades ago.

I have talked about the gap between our aspirations and our achievements, about the need to achieve black economic empowerment, about the need to implement affirmative action programs that help us to meet that goal. And I have talked about the South's re-entry into the nation's political life, and removing the burden of race from our region's and our nation's life.

As we consider the sweep of time and look to the future, we can better understand that only by constructing an open, pluralistic, integrated society can America survive into the twenty-first century. Only by overcoming the inequalities that still permeate our society can we build a nation whose decency matches its prosperity, and whose unity propels it to new, higher levels of accomplishment.

And in the struggle to reach for the heights of a better society, each and every one of us must play a constructive role. Each of us must reach out to others; each of us must overcome the artificial barriers of class and race to assert our humanity and our solidarity with our citizens of our national family.

Finishing the Task

We began that great adventure in the civil rights era of the 1960s. And now it is our task . . . to complete that great adventure of the American spirit.

Four hundred years ago, the great English adventurer Sir Francis Drake wrote, "It isn't the beginning of the task, but the continuing of the same until it be well and truly finished wherein lies the true glory."

"When patterns of discrimination are apparent, affirmative action and quotas may be valid tools to respond."

Racial Quotas Protect the Rights of Minorities

Douglas B. Huron

Since the passage of the Civil Rights Act of 1964, the Supreme Court has yet to issue a clear-cut ruling on whether quotas should be used to protect the rights of minorities. In the following viewpoint, Douglas B. Huron argues in favor of affirmative action and quotas. He states that in cases where past discrimination against minorities is a problem, race-balancing solutions may be required. Huron is a former senior trial attorney in the Justice Department, Civil Rights Division. He was senior associate counsel to former President Jimmy Carter and is now a practicing lawyer in Washington, DC.

As you read, consider the following questions:

1. How do affirmative action goals within a company benefit minorities, according to Huron?
2. Why does Huron believe that court sanctioned racial quotas are sometimes the only way to achieve results?
3. According to Huron, what should be included to make an affirmative action program an effective weapon against discrimination?

Douglas B. Huron, "Racial Quotas Protect the Rights of Minorities," *Human Rights*, Fall 1985. Reprinted with permission.

It may be fashionable to insist that affirmative action, and especially quotas for minorities, don't work. But not for the first time, the fashion is wrong. In many kinds of situations these remedies do work, providing job opportunities for qualified (or easily qualifiable) people who otherwise would not have them.

This does not mean we should turn to affirmative action to solve all the problems of America's unemployed and underemployed minorities. Affirmative action provides useful tools, not panaceas. Affirmative action cannot make an illiterate person literate, or teach good work habits, or turn someone with janitor's skills into an engineer. There is no substitute for education, training and apprenticeship.

Supreme Court Rulings

It is clear that the White House, through the Justice Department, opposes any race-related quotas or goals for hiring or promotion of public workers. Although the Supreme Court last year, in the *Stotts* decision, upheld the seniority rights of a group of white firefighters in Memphis, it has not decided whether a racially based formula for public hiring is illegal and unconstitutional.

The Court has now agreed to review a Michigan ruling that upholds an affirmative action plan calling for layoffs of nonminority teachers who have more experience than some minority teachers, but are being laid off in order for the staff to maintain a racial balance.

The [Reagan] administration is arguing that the Supreme Court's ruling in *Stotts* sets the stage for striking down all preferential quotas in hiring and promoting public workers. Recently, the Justice Department has gone to court in a number of cities to overturn hiring agreements that contain racial quotas.

A Need for Quotas

In many circumstances, members of minority groups have been discriminated against casually, thoughtlessly—because it has been the fashion not to hire them. Thus, many big city police and fire departments traditionally hired no blacks; many craft unions accepted no blacks as members; many big companies put no blacks in positions higher than kitchen help and janitors. When patterns of discrimination are apparent, affirmative action and quotas may be valid tools to respond. And they may also be useful for an employer who recognizes the problem and wants to change it voluntarily.

The utility of affirmative action and quotas was demonstrated in 1983 in hearings held by Reps. Don Edwards (D-Cal.) and Patricia Schroeder (D-Colo.). In those hearings I talked about public sector employment in Alabama, something I learned about as an attorney in the Justice Department's civil rights division in the Nixon-Ford administration. Another witness at the same hearings was Fred Cook, vice president for human resources at Mountain Bell in Denver.

Alabama has seen dramatic changes in the level and type of black employment in public agencies over the past decade. Most of that change is directly attributable to litigation and specifically to affirmative action and quota decrees entered by Judge Frank Johnson of Montgomery. And it is tough to imagine how blacks would have gotten those state jobs in Alabama without them.

Entrenched Racism

In the late 1960s, the 70-odd Alabama state agencies employed only a handful of blacks above the menial level. At that time the Justice Department sued seven of the larger agencies which together employed over half the state government's work force. Following trial, Judge Johnson found that of the 1,000 clerical employees in these agencies, only one was black. Of over 2,000 workers in semiprofessional and supervisory positions, just 26 were black.

Affirmative Action Works

By all accounts, affirmative action has been a success. Studies done for the Labor Department concluded that goals and timetables have been instrumental in bringing minority members and women into the workforce in increasing numbers.

If today's approach to affirmative action has flaws, let's fix it, not abandon it. No one wants Federal contractors to be subject to excessive and onerous paperwork burdens. No one believes that people should be chosen strictly on their race or sex, or without regard to qualifications.

Justice Harry A. Blackmun of the United States Supreme Court once said that to get beyond racism, we must first take account of race. It is simplistic and naive to think that in just 20 years, our nation has broken down all of the race and sex discrimination barriers that for so long excluded so many people from opportunities. A color-blind society is still a dream, not a reality. Saving affirmative action will help the nation move closer to that goal.

Don Edwards, *The New York Times*, February 13, 1986.

This paucity of black employees was no accident, since the state refused to recruit at black schools and in black media and also maintained segregated cafeteria facilities.

Even more telling, on those occasions when black applicants appeared at the top of employment registers, agencies simply passed over them in favor of low-ranked whites.

To try to remedy these entrenched discriminatory patterns,

Judge Johnson enjoined the passing-over of qualified blacks and required the state to attempt to recruit black applicants. He also ordered the hiring of some 62 blacks who had been passed over and who could be identified following a laborious process of records analysis. In short, Frank Johnson in 1970 ordered everything W. Bradford Reynolds, the current assistant attorney general for civil fights, would require of an employer guilty of discrimination.

But nothing substantive changed, despite Alabama's compliance with the specific elements of Judge Johnson's decree. Perhaps the state's attitude was still too grudging, or blacks were still too skeptical, or perhaps other factors were at work. Whatever the explanation, black employment in Alabama agencies remained low.

The one exception to this otherwise gloomy picture lay in the area of temporary employment. There Johnson had simply imposed a ratio—a quota—on temporary hires. The ratio was fixed at 25 percent—approximately the black population percentage in Alabama—and the goal was met. But there was still no improvement in permanent positions.

Alabama's Turning Point

Then in January 1972, the Alabama NAACP filed suit against the Department of Public Safety—the state troopers. At that time everyone in Public Safety was white—the troopers, the officers and the support personnel. No blacks had ever been employed there. Throughout the '50s and '60s—from the school-house door to the Selma bridge—the troopers had been the most visible instrument defending segregation.

Judge Johnson set an early trial date, then ruled from the bench, finding that Public Safety had engaged in a "blatant and continuous pattern and practice of discrimination." Having learned from his experience with the other Alabama agencies, Johnson immediately imposed a quota: he required the state to hire one black trooper for each new white hired, until blacks reached 25 percent of the trooper force. He also applied the same formula to support personnel.

The state complied, and the results have been little short of astounding. Within weeks, Alabama had hired its first black troopers. Within two years, there were a substantial number of blacks on the force, and the director of Public Safety later testified that they were competent professionals.

[In 1985], 13 years after the entry of Judge Johnson's decree, Alabama has the most thoroughly integrated state police force in the country. Over 20 percent of the troopers and officers—and nearly 25 percent of the support personnel—are black. The day is fast approaching when Public Safety will be freed of hiring constraints. And although 13 years may seem a long time for a court order to remain in effect, the problem was years longer in the making.

When Justice contrasted the initial results on the trooper force with the lack of progress in other Alabama agencies, the department went back into court, asking that hiring ratios be applied to entry-level jobs in the other Alabama agencies. Judge Johnson gave the agencies plenty of time—over two years—to mend their ways.

Producing Results

When little changed, he issued a decision finding statewide discrimination, but he demurred to Justice's plea for quotas. He said that "mandatory hiring quotas must be a last resort," and he declined to order them. But he noted that the denial would be "without prejudice" to Justice's seeking the same relief one year later: "In the event substantial progress has not been made by the 70 state agencies, hiring goals will then be the only alternative."

Racial Quotas Create Substantive Equality

I have never met anyone who wants to alter the Constitution, who says that he wants racial quotas forever. But until society is willing to do something to change the historical affirmative action for whites and bring blacks into the system, there will be affirmative action. The American people may not understand or may be unwilling to be bored by historians, lawyers, and political scientists arguing high theory, but they understand that our society has been discriminating against nonwhites, that it continues to do so, that it has got to change, and that affirmative action may be the way to change it. . . .

The more the American people get used to the idea that blacks can wear police uniforms too, the less resistant they will be and the more likely it is that we can achieve what I think is the original intention and the overarching goal of the three civil-rights amendments: to create substantive equality for all people in this country.

Paul Finkelman, *The Center Magazine*, November/December 1987.

The message—the threat—could not have been clearer, and the agencies immediately began to come around. In the eight largest departments, which together account for close to 75 percent of all state workers, black employment increased by over half between 1975 and 1983 and now stands at over 20 percent. And black workers, who used to be concentrated in menial jobs, now appear in substantial numbers in nearly all the larger job categories.

No doubt problems remain in Alabama, but the only fair conclusion is that dramatic progress has been achieved in public employment for blacks over the past decade. And in view of the history of the Alabama litigation, it is clear that this would not have occurred if Judge Johnson had not first imposed a hiring quota on the state troopers—and then threatened to extend it statewide if the other agencies did not alter their discriminatory practices.

At Mountain Bell—an affiliate of AT&T before divestiture—affirmative action was also needed. In 1972, AT&T entered into a six-year consent decree with the EEOC [Equal Employment Opportunity Commission] and the Justice Department to substantially increase the number of minority and female workers, as well as the number of women in non-traditional jobs such as installers, cable repairers and frame attendants.

Focusing Company Efforts

It was not easy at first. Fred Cook said Mountain Bell did not meet its goals for the first year of the decree, but the company then intensified its recruiting efforts and was on target for the next five. As a result, minority managers at the company have increased from under 200 to over 1,400, and there are now nearly 1,200 women in non-traditional jobs, compared to 81 in the year before the decree.

Cook defends Mountain Bell's employment practices in the '50s and '60s, saying that his company was more responsive than most to the aspirations of minorities and female workers. But, he frankly admits that the consent decree focused the company's efforts in a particularly acute and compelling way. As he put it, "It became as important as the bottom line." If it weren't for the decree, with its affirmative action goals, the progress Cook recounted would not have been made.

Uncovering Talent

It is also significant that affirmative action has helped Mountain Bell in a very practical way. Fred Cook said recently that, before the consent decree, "we were reflecting society. We were not using all the talent available." Under the decree, though, the company discovered that its minority and female work force was a "gold mine" for high-quality managers.

And in the wake of Mountain Bell's own efforts, blacks, Hispanics, and women formed organizations aimed at helping one another and at assisting the company in identifying still more talent. Cook praised the work of these groups, and he said that the net result is that Mountain Bell has done a "very good job, especially since the consent decree has ended." The company has no interest in turning back. According to Cook, "it is good business sense to take this kind of affirmative action." It is ironic that it took government action to sharpen Bell's business judgment.

Affirmative action can be a potent weapon, so it should be used only with great care. An effective affirmative action program should have a limited duration, should be aimed only at genuine problems caused by past discrimination, and should not lower standards. Otherwise the problem of selection based on race or sex may be perpetuated indefinitely.

The Litmus Test of Civil Rights

Affirmative action is the litmus test of civil rights.

Affirmative action . . . works for states and cities that complied with court orders to hire minorities and women for jobs in city services, in police stations, in fire houses.

It works for companies that hired blacks to have respectable numbers to show, and then concluded that affirmative action is just good business.

Race-conscious remedies are needed to correct the evils of a race-conscious past. No one can look at the history of discrimination without a sense of shame. And no one can suppose we can correct that history without aggressive affirmative action programs, both public and private.

John E. Jacob, speech delivered at the Annual Conference of the National Urban League, Inc., Washington, DC, July 21, 1985.

In deciding whether affirmative action is desirable or required, the key question is, what caused a company to exclude blacks from its work force, or keep them in menial jobs? When the answer is that blacks did not have the requisite skills or training, then affirmative action is unlikely to be an effective remedy.

But when the cause is discrimination, whether it is overt or casual discrimination, affirmative action may then be required.

"Ultimately, quotas will be the bane of minorities."

Racial Quotas Threaten the Rights of Minorities

Robert J. Bresler

Robert J. Bresler is chairman of the Public Policy Program at Pennsylvania State University and national affairs editor of *USA Today*. In the following viewpoint, Bresler argues against the use of quotas to remedy past problems of discrimination. Quotas are harmful, Bresler contends, because the size and strength of a group will become the determining factor in their distribution. Thus, the rights of minority groups will in the end lose to those of white males.

As you read, consider the following questions:

1. Bresler states that the court rulings in discrimination cases are unclear. What examples does he cite to support his claim?
2. How do racial quotas undermine the constitution's understanding of rights, according to the author?
3. Why does Bresler believe that white males will maintain their predominance if group rights are sanctioned?

There is a tendency among democratic societies to avoid a clear-cut resolution of basic conflicts. Rather than resolving an issue one way or the other, democracies often prefer to muddle through and to avoid antagonizing one side or the other. So it is with affirmative action. Going back to the celebrated *Bakke* case in 1978, the Supreme Court has steadily refused to give an unambiguous answer to the question of whether race-conscious remedies such as quotas are a permissible means of redressing discrimination.

A Confusing Decision

In *Bakke*, Justice Lewis Powell, writing the judgment of the Court, declared that the University of California-Davis Medical School could not set aside a specific number of spaces in its entering class exclusively for minorities. However, the Medical School *could* consider race a "plus" in a minority candidate's application file. Powell cited the Harvard College admission program as a model. The distinction between having an outright quota for minorities and adding a set number of points to the admission rating of a minority applicant eluded many, including Justice Harry Blackmun, who commented that, "Harvards' [programs] may accomplish covertly] what Davis concedes it does openly." What the Court actually resolved in *Bakke* remains unclear. It struck down the Davis quota system, but did not preclude some form of race-conscious remedies.

The next year, the Court actually embraced a quota system. In *United Steelworkers v. Weber* (1979), it approved a collective-bargaining agreement that reserved 50% of the openings in a skilled-worker-training program for blacks. Ralph Weber was a white member of the union who was passed over for one of the skilled-labor positions in favor of a black. The Court cited that Title VII of the Civil Rights Act of 1964, which bans racial discrimination in employment, did not prohibit "all voluntary private, race-conscious efforts to abolish traditional patterns" of discrimination.

Destroying the Notion of Equality

This majority opinion, written by Justice William Brennan, seemed to ignore the explicit legislative history of the landmark 1964 law. In *Freedom and the Court*, Prof. Henry J. Abraham cites a statement by the bill's floor manager, Sen. Hubert H. Humphrey, who told one of the bill's opponents during the Senate debate that, "If the Senator can find in Title VII . . . any language which provides that an employer will have to hire on the basis of percentage or quota related to color . . . I will start eating the pages, one after another, because it is not there." Justice William Rehnquist, in a blistering dissent in *Weber*, said that Brennan's decision was "reminiscent not of jurists such as Hale, Holmes and Hughes, but

Don Hesse for the *St. Louis Globe-Democrat.*

of escape artists such as Houdini." Rehnquist insisted that "there is perhaps no device more destructive to the notion of equality than . . . the quota. Whether described as 'benign discrimination' or 'affirmative action,' the racial quota is nonetheless a control of castes, a two-edged sword that must demean one in order to prefer the other."

Following *Weber*, which approved a racial quota that was voluntary and temporary, the Court, in a subsequent case, gave the concept even greater legitimacy. In *Fullilove v. Klutznick,* the Court approved a Congressional law which set aside 10% of a $4,000,000,000 public works program for Minority Business Enterprises (MBE's), which were defined as companies in which blacks, Hispanic-Americans, Oriental-Americans, American Indians, Eskimos, or Aleuts controlled at least 50% interest. The Court, speaking through Chief Justice Warren Burger, rejected the idea that "Congress is obligated to act in a wholly 'color-blind' fashion." Racial quotas could be employed by Congress so long as they were "narrowly tailored" to remedy past discrimination. Justice Potter Stewart's dissent was no less vehement than was Rehnquist's in *Weber.* Stewart, who steadfastly adhered to Justice Harlan's maxim in *Plessy v. Ferguson* that "Our Constitution is color-blind," lamented that the Court had "place[d] its imprimatur on the creation once again by government of privileges based on birth."

Whites as Victims

Taking their cues from the Supreme Court, lower courts began fashioning consent decrees that established clear racial quotas in hiring and promotions. In *Firefighters v. Stotts* (1984), the Supreme Court made a sharp departure from its previous decisions, ruling that white firefighters were unjustly laid off in favor of black firefighters with less seniority who had been hired as part of a court-ordered affirmative action decree. Justice Byron White, speaking for the majority in this case, stated that a race-conscious remedy can only apply to the actual "victims of discriminatory practice." Seniority, White argued, could be violated only to assist a specifically identified victim of discrimination. Was White saying that all racial quotas reward those who were not the individual victims of discrimination and, therefore, are no longer valid? Or, was White referring only to court-ordered racial quotas which violated *bona fide* seniority systems?

William Bradford Reynolds, the Assistant Attorney General for Civil Rights, interpreted White's opinion in the broadest way. He argued that *Stotts* "precludes persons who are not actual victims of discrimination from receiving preferential treatment." Lower Federal courts, on the other hand, have steadfastly refused to accept Reynolds' broad reading of *Stotts* and have upheld the use of numerical goals and racial quotas in cases that do not involve minority systems or layoffs. . . .

Group Rights vs. Individual Rights

Few issues in contemporary American life come closer to the very meaning of our political tradition. Theodore White has written that the strategy of black leaders who champion affirmative action has been "to transform the traditional credo of American politics 'equality' into the credo of 'group equality' . . . what blacks want most is public acceptance of equality, not only on the basis of individual merit, but the group results and group shares." In the same spirit, many feminists and homosexual activists claim that their rights are rooted in their identity as gays or women. It is one thing to say that all have certain rights regardless of race, creed, or color, and another to say that one has rights as a black, a woman, or a homosexual. The first position considers rights to be individually based; the second considers rights to be rooted in some group membership. Racial quotas or gender quotas legitimize the concept of group rights and, for that reason, raise profound questions about the nature of American constitutional values.

Quotas Undermine Civil Rights

Whites want to maintain their high standard of living; Blacks want an equal standard of living. The present attempts to solve the problem can be found in civil rights initiatives, mostly laws approved by the white majority intended to secure constitutional guarantees and an equal standard of living.

But affirmative programs—especially quotas, which were meant to increase Black employment—became particularly irksome to Whites. As a result, many now view the entire civil rights thrust as preferential treatment, and they oppose any further legislation on that basis.

Many Whites oppose, implicitly anyway, the aspirations of Blacks out of self-interest, not necessarily racism. But whether the motive is vested self-interest or racial self-interest, it is opposition of the ruling majority based on the desire to maintain a high standard of living that they feel is being jeopardized by undeserving beneficiaries.

Eventually, this opinion works its way through the system. Finally, the Constitution is whatever the politicians—including the President—who reflect White-majority public opinion and the Supreme Court say it is.

Tony Brown, speech delivered to the Commonwealth Club of California, San Francisco, California, February 20, 1987.

The weight of American history seems, to this writer, to stand clearly on the side of individual rights. Group rights carry the memory of a white-dominated caste system which Abraham Lincoln sought to end. As Lincoln put it, the cause of the Union was to maintain "in the world that form and substance of a government whose leading object is to evaluate the condition of men— to lift the artificial weights from all shoulders, to clear the paths of laudable pursuit for all, to afford all an unfettered start, and a fair chance in the race of life . . . this is the leading object of the government for whose existence we contend." The Civil War Amendments (the Thirteenth, Fourteenth, and Fifteenth), ratified after Lincoln's death, reaffirmed his vision of our Republic. All persons were granted rights regardless of race. Rights were rooted not in race, but in citizenship, and citizenship was granted to "*all* persons born or naturalized in the United States" (Amendment XIV, Sec. 1). These Amendments made it clear that the Constitution recognized no system of caste.

A Weapon in the Hands of Many

Rights, personal and individual, were placed in the Constitution beyond the reach of an ordinary majority and simple legislative whim. Racial quotas strike at the heart of this constitutional understanding of rights. First, they are based upon group status and, eventually, group influence. Second, they establish the precedent that one's rights are subject to the pushing and shoving of the ordinary political process, not the extraodinary constitutional process. Once quotas are sanctioned, how will they equitably be distributed? Over time, rights could become politicized, with each group entitled only to those rights that they can secure politically. If one's right to a job or a place in a professional school is no longer based upon individual merit, we begin a slide down a treacherous slope. At first, these opportunities may go to those groups who claim a historic grievance. Eventually, however, they will go to those with political muscle. For example, since Asian-Americans and Jewish-Americans make up a disproportionate number of our university faculties, will those numbers have to be reduced at some point in the future to reflect their actual percentage of the population? The Civil Rights Revolution and, for that matter, the American Revolution will then be placed on their heads. Our classic struggles—for self-government in the late-18th century, against slavery in the mid-19th, and for civil rights in the mid-20th—all affirmed the principle that each should be allowed to rise as far as his talents and efforts will take him. . . .

Ultimately, quotas will be the bane of minorities. If group rights are sanctioned, group strength will determine the disposition of those rights. Minorities, not white males, will be the losers. As Justice Rehnquist reminded us, quotas are a two-edged sword. Today, that sword may swing to protect the few, but tomorrow it may be a weapon in the hands of many. On no other issue is the Bible's admonishment more apt, "for whatsoever a man soweth, that he shall also reap."

Distinguishing Bias from Reason

When dealing with controversial issues, many people allow their feelings to dominate their powers of reason. Thus, one of the most important critical thinking skills is the ability to distinguish between statements based upon emotion or bias and conclusions based upon a rational consideration of the facts.

The following statements are taken from the viewpoints in this chapter. Consider each statement carefully. *Mark R for any statement you believe is based on reason or a rational consideration of the facts. Mark B for any statement you believe is based on bias, prejudice, or emotion. Mark I for any statement you think is impossible to judge.*

If you are doing this activity as a member of a class or group, compare your answers with those of other class or group members. Be able to defend your answers. You may discover that others come to different conclusions than you do. Listening to the rationale others present for their answers may give you valuable insights in distinguishing between bias and reason.

R = a statement based upon reason
B = a statement based upon bias
I = a statement impossible to judge

216

1. Alabama has seen a dramatic change in black employment in public agencies, mostly due to affirmative action and quotas. Considering the state's history of discriminatory hiring practices, it is tough to imagine how blacks would have gotten those state jobs without litigation.

2. There is perhaps no device more destructive to the notion of equality than the quota.

3. Many blacks believe they are due a special preference from the government to make up for the despicable institution of slavery. They are wrong.

4. Affirmative action can destroy the dignity of minorities and tends to create resentment among others. It undermines persons' ability to prove themselves capable of achieving without government help.

5. The large number of civil rights court cases before the Supreme Court in the last decade proves that discrimination remains a stubborn factor in American society.

6. Many black leaders are out to change the traditional American meaning of "equality" to mean "group equality." Their strategy is to transform the constitutional meaning of individual-based rights to mean the recognition of group rights.

7. There is much that black people can do for themselves, but national policies can provide employment and training opportunities that make self-help efforts feasible.

8. If the government does not educate its neglected minorities, America can soon expect second-class economic status and deep unrest at home.

9. Washington's policies always served social ends. The government bailed out Chrysler. It should play an equally decisive role in providing opportunities that protect black rights and reduce poverty.

10. After two decades of civil rights efforts, more than three-fourths of the children born in inner-city ghettos are born out of wedlock and black high school dropout rates in Chicago and Detroit are near 50 percent. Thus, not all of the problems facing blacks can be eliminated through civil rights policies.

Periodical Bibliography

The following articles have been selected to supplement the diverse views presented in this chapter.

Harry S. Ashmore, Patricia Derian, and M. Carl Holman
"The Movement's Unfinished Business Is a Tough Agenda," *The New York Times*, August 28, 1983.

Derrick Bell
"To Make a Nation Whole," *The New York Times Magazine*, September 13, 1987.

Derek Bok
"Goals Aren't Quotas," *The Washington Post*, March 10, 1986.

Nancy A. Boxill and Creigs C. Beverly
"A Black Self-Help Development Program," *Social Policy*, Spring 1986.

Central Committee, CPUSA
"On Afro-American Equality," *Political Affairs*, April 1987.

Claudia H. Deutsch
"Still on the Outside Looking In," *The New York Times*, July 5, 1987.

Richard A. Epstein
"Affirmative Reaction," *The New Republic*, October 12, 1987.

Harvard Journal of Law and Public Policy
"The 1985 Federalist Society National Meeting: A Symposium," Winter 1986.

John E. Jacob
"A Society That Is Just and Fair," *Vital Speeches of the Day*, September 15, 1987.

Charles Krauthammer
"Muddling Through, Wisely, on Racial Bias," *Los Angeles Times*, June 9, 1986.

James Nuechterlein
"A Farewell to Civil Rights," *Commentary*, August 1987.

Victor Reisel
"When Goals Become Quotas," *The Washington Times*, Jaurary 21, 1986.

William Bradford Reynolds
"Non-Discrimination Polices Should Apply to *All*", *Human Events*, November 30, 1985.

Cal Thomas
"A Time for All of Us To Join Hands," *The Washington Times*, January 31, 1986.

Juan Williams
"Racism Revisited," *Utne Reader*, May/June 1987.

Walter E. Williams
"Civil Rightspeak," *New Perspectives*, Winter/Spring 1986.

Organizations To Contact

The editors have compiled the following list of organizations concerned with the issues debated in this book. All of them have publications available for interested readers. The descriptions are derived from materials provided by the organizations themselves.

Affirmative Action Coordinating Center
126 W. 119th St.
New York, NY 10026
(212) 864-4000

The Center coordinates a network of organizations that believe affirmative action programs are both legal and necessary for overcoming the effects of discrimination. It acts as a clearinghouse and resource center for materials concerning policies and court actions on affirmative action programs. It also provides resources for developing legal intervention strategies for affirmative action. It publishes the quarterly *News*.

American Civil Liberties Union (ACLU)
National Headquarters
132 W. 43rd St.
New York, NY 10036
(212) 944-9800

The ACLU is a very active national organization with many local chapters. It champions human rights as guaranteed in the Declaration of Independence and the Constitution, including freedom of inquiry and expression, due process of law and fair trials, and equality before the law. Its activities include test cases, opposition to repressive legislation, and public protest of attacks on constitutional and human rights. It publishes a wealth of materials on civil liberties, including the *ACLU Policy Guide*, *Civil Liberties*, and *Our Endangered Rights*.

American Library Association
Office of Intellectual Freedom
50 E. Huron St.
Chicago, IL 60611
(312) 944-6780

The Office of Intellectual Freedom is a resource for the public on the issues of free speech, free inquiry, and freedom of the press. It also seeks to promote the recognition and acceptance of libraries and to protect the public's right of access to them. It publishes brochures and a monthly *Newsletter on Intellectual Freedom*.

Americans United for Separation of Church and State
8120 Fenton St.
Silver Spring, MD 20910
(301) 589-3707

This organization's purpose is to protect the right of Americans to religious freedom. Its principal means of action are litigation, education, and advocacy. It opposes the passing of both state and federal laws which threaten the separation of church and state. Its many publications include brochures, pamphlets, and a monthly newsletter, *Church and State*.

219

Anti-Repression Resource Team
PO Box 122
Jackson, MS 39205
(601) 969-2269

The Team fights against all forms of political repression, including police brutality, Nazi and Ku Klux Klan terrorism, and spying on citizens by intelligence agencies. Its activities include writing, lecturing, organizing, and conducting training workshops for church, labor, and community groups. It also maintains a library and a speakers bureau. It publishes a pamphlet entitled *The New State Repression*.

Center for National Policy Review
1025 Vermont Ave. NW, Suite 360
Washington, DC 20005
(202) 783-5640

The Center conducts nonpartisan research and reviews of national urban and racial policies. Its main objective is to aid civil rights and public interest groups in presenting their concerns to government agencies. The Center has five divisions: Education, Employment, Federal Programs, Housing, and Minority Enterprise. Its publications include the bimonthly *Jobs Watch*, and an annual report.

Christian Action Council
701 W. Broad St., Suite 405
Falls Church, VA 22046
(703) 237-2100

The Council is a group of Christians committed to the principle that law and public policy in our country should be in harmony with fundamental Biblical principles. It encourages Christians to get politically involved and to persuade lawmakers to heed fundamental Biblical values. It is also committed to getting an anti-abortion amendment passed by Congress. Its publications include numerous brochures and the monthly *Action Line*.

Christian Voice
214 Massachusetts Ave. NE, Suite 120
Washington, DC 20002
(202) 544-5202

The Voice is a major Christian lobbying organization. The group seeks to restore traditional Christian values throughout the country. Its goals include the return of school prayer, the banning of pornography, and preventing the passing of gay rights and abortion laws. It publishes many brochures, books, the monthly *Legislative Alert*, and the annual *Congressional Report Card*.

Citizens for Decency Through Law
11000 N. Scotsdale Rd., Suite 210
Phoenix, AZ 85254
(602) 995-2600

The group's purpose is to help legislatures and law inforcement agencies enact and enforce laws controlling obscenity and pornography. It works to create public awareness of the dangers and harm associated with pornography in the media and arts. It also provides free legal assistance in obscenity and pornography cases. Its publications include brochures and the bimonthly, *The CDL Reporter*.

Citizens for Educational Freedom
1611 N. Kent St., #805
Arlington, VA 22209
(703) 524-1991

The group is made up of parents and other individuals who proclaim the right to choose the type of education they desire for their children. It seeks alternatives to the public school system and tax benefits for non-public educational systems and methods. It publishes a bimonthly, *Freedom in Education* and the semiannual *Educational Freedom*.

Constitutional Rights Foundation
PO Box 2362
Texas City, TX 77592
(713) 460-3030

The Foundation's purpose is to help people protect themselves from civil rights abuses by the Internal Revenue Service. It also teaches citizens how to protect property rights and how to represent oneself in court. It maintains a library, a speakers bureau, and a computer service. Its publications include the monthly journal, *The American*, and the books, *More Than a Tax Revolt* and *W-4: The Battle Plan*.

Eagle Forum
Box 618
Alton, IL 62002
(618) 462-5415

The Forum is a politically-active group that advocates traditional Biblical values. It opposes the Equal Rights Amendment and seeks increases in tax exemptions for children. It fights against political forces it sees as anti-family, anti-religion, anti-life, and anti-morality. It publishes the monthly *Phyllis Schlafly Report*, and the Eagle Forum *Newsletter*.

International Committee Against Racism
PO Box 904 GPO
Brooklyn, NY 11202
(718) 287-4325

The Committee is dedicated to fighting all forms of racism and to building a multi-racial society. It opposes economic, social, institutional, and cultural forms of racism. It sponsors workshops for high school and college students. It also publishes a monthly newsletter, *Arrow*.

Mental Health Law Project
2021 L St. NW, Suite 800
Washington, DC 20036
(202) 467-5730

The Project's purpose is to clarify, establish, and enforce the legal rights of mentally and developmentally disabled persons. It has developed a mental health legislative guide. Its staff attorneys have worked on many landmark court cases that have established the rights of the mentally disabled. It publishes a bimonthly newsletter, *The Mental Health Law Project's Update* and *ALERT*, a quarterly.

Morality in Media, Inc.
475 Riverside Dr.
New York, NY 10115
(212) 870-3222

This organization opposes pornography and indecency in media and encourages more vigorous enforcement of obscenity laws. It does not believe in censorship or prior restraint by the government. It publishes the monthly *Morality in Media Newsletter*, *Hill-Link Report of the Presidential Commission on Obscenity and Pornography*, and pamphlets, including *You Can Help Stop the Pornography Traffic*.

Moral Majority
305 6th St.
Lynchburg, VA 24504
(804) 528-5000

The Moral Majority is a political movement dedicated to convincing morally conservative Americans that it is their duty to register and vote for candidates who agree with their moral principles. The movement opposes legalized abortion, pornography, and gay rights. It publishes a monthly newspaper, *Report*.

National Alliance Against Racist and Political Repression
126 W. 119th St., Suite 101
New York, NY 10026
(212) 866-8600

This coalition of political, labor, church, civic, and student organizations is dedicated to protecting people's right to organize. It opposes government persecution of groups and individuals seeking social change, including illegal aliens, prison inmates, draft resisters, and militant students. It produces audiovisual programs and publishes pamphlets and a quarterly newsletter, *The Organizer*.

National Association for the Advancement of Colored People (NAACP)
186 Remsen St.
Brooklyn, NY 11201
(212) 858-0800

Founded in 1909, the NAACP works through the democratic process to achieve equal rights and to eliminate racial prejudice. It tries to remove racial discrimination from all political, social, business, and cultural institutions. It publishes an annual report and a monthly newsletter, *Crisis*.

National Association of Property Owners
2400 Tower Life Building
San Antonio, TX 78205
(512) 226-2331

The Association is a public interest organization dedicated to protecting the interests of private property owners. It believes that property ownership is essential to the preservation of individual liberty and a free republic. It opposes federal land acquisition, excessive taxation of property, and environmental laws which take land out of production. It publishes the monthly *Your Property Newsletter*.

National Committee for Sexual Civil Liberties
18 Ober Rd.
Princeton, NJ 08540
(609) 924-1950

This organization works to break down the structure of prejudice which surrounds private sexual conduct between consenting adults. It also calls for the repeal of all laws punishing fornication, sodomy, adultery, and pornography involving adults. It publishes a quarterly, *Sexual Law Reporter*.

National Council on Religion and Public Education
1300 Oread Ave.
Lawrence, KS 66045
(913) 843-7257

The Council helps other organizations that want to find ways to study religion in a public school setting. It publishes *Religion and Public Education* magazine as well as many pamphlets and brochures.

National Gay Task Force
80 5th Ave.
New York, NY 10011
(212) 741-5800

The Task Force is dedicated to eliminating prejudice against persons based on their sexual orientation. It lobbies for equal rights for gay and lesbian citizens, works with the media on eliminating sex role stereotyping, and assists other organizations in working effectively with the gay and lesbian community. It publishes the bimonthly *Task Force Report* and packets of support statements on gay civil rights, as well as numerous booklets and pamphlets.

National Justice Foundation of America
1617 16th St.
Sacramento, CA 95814
(916) 442-0537

The Foundation believes in the ownership of private property and a constitutional republic. It promotes the right to bear arms, fair taxation, and freedom of choice in matters of health, education, and business association. It publishes special reports as well as the *Highlights Sheet Quarterly*.

National Lawyers Guild
853 Broadway, Suite 1705
New York, NY 10003
(212) 260-1360

The Guild refers to itself as "the conscience of the bar in the United States." Its aim is to bring together all those who look upon the law as an instrument for the protection of people rather than for their repression. It is active in every sphere of social justice. It publishes a national newspaper, *Guild Notes*, as well as a list of its many other publications.

National Urban League
500 E. 62nd St.
New York, NY 10021
(212) 310-9000

The Urban League is a large voluntary community service organization. Its aims are to eliminate racial segregation, discrimination, and institutional racism. It publishes a quarterly, *The Urban League News* and the seminannual *The Urban League Review*.

People for the American Way
2000 M St. NW, Suite 400
Washington, DC 20036
(202) 467-4999

The aim of this organization is to continue the American tradition of diversity and pluralism. It opposes groups that seek to use religion and religious symbols for political purposes to create a divisive atmosphere of intolerance and bigotry. Its many publications include a monthly, *News from People for the American Way* and an annual, *Attacks on the Freedom To Learn*.

Southern Christian Leadership Conference (SCLC)
334 Auburn Ave. NE
Atlanta, GA 30312
(404) 522-1420

The SCLC is a nonsectarian coordinating and service agency for local civil rights organizations. It works to establish full citizenship rights and integration of blacks and subscribes to Gandhi's principle of nonviolence. It trains community leaders in nonviolent forms of protest and civil rights. It has been instrumental in encouraging blacks to register to vote. It publishes the monthly *Newsletter*.

United States Commission on Civil Rights
1121 Vermont Ave. NW
Washington, DC 20425
(202) 376-8177

The Commission is a fact-finding body that makes recommendations directly to the President and Congress. It evaluates federal laws and the effectiveness of equal opportunity programs. It also serves as a national clearinghouse for civil rights information. A catalog of its publications is available from the Publications Management Division at the above address.

Book Bibliography

Mortimer J. Adler	*We Hold These Truths.* New York: Macmillan, 1987.
American Civil Liberties Union	*Why the American Civil Liberties Union Defends Free Speech for Racists and Totalitarians.* New York: American Civil Liberties Union. Pamphlet available from the ACLU, 132 W. 43rd St., New York, NY 10036.
Attorney General's Commission on Pornography	*Final Report of the Attorney General's Commission on Pornography.* Washington, DC: US Government Printing Office, 1986.
Derrick Bell	*And We Are Not Saved: The Elusive Search for Racial Justice.* New York: Basic Books, 1987.
Clint Bolick	*Changing Course: Civil Rights at the Crossroads.* New Brunswick, NJ: Transaction Books, 1988.
Lee C. Bollinger	*The Tolerant Society: Freedom of Speech and Extremist Speech in America.* New York: Oxford University Press, 1986.
Theodore Cross	*The Black Power Imperative—Racial Inequality and the Power of Nonviolence.* New York: Faulkner Books, 1984.
Harold Cruse	*Plural But Equal.* New York: William Morrow and Company, Inc., 1987.
Norman Dorsen, ed.	*Our Endangered Rights: The ACLU Report on Civil Rights Today.* New York: Pantheon Books, 1984.
Donald Alexander Downs	*Nazis in Skokie: Freedom, Community, and the First Amendment.* Notre Dame, IN: University of Notre Dame Press, 1985.
Robert B. Downs & Ralph E. McCoy, eds.	*The First Freedom Today: Critical Issues Relating to Censorship and to Intellectual Freedom.* Chicago: American Library Association, 1984.
Margaret Edds	*Free at Last: What Really Happened When Civil Rights Came to Southern Politics.* Bethesda, MD: Adler & Adler, 1987.
James K. Fitzpatrick	*God, Country, and the Supreme Court.* Chicago: Regnery Books, 1985.
Lois G. Forer	*A Chilling Effect: The Mounting Threat of Libel and Invasion of Privacy Actions to the First Amendment.* New York: W.W. Norton and Company, 1987.
Jerry Fresia	*We the People: Confronting the Failures of the Constitution.* Boston: South End Press, 1987.
Stephen Goode	*The Right to Privacy.* New York: Franklin Watts, 1983.
Richard F. Hixson	*Privacy in a Public Society.* New York: Oxford University Press, 1987.
Dorothy and Thomas Hoobler	*Your Right to Privacy.* New York: Franklin Watts, 1986.
Carl Horn, ed.	*Whose Values? The Battle for Morality in Pluralistic America.* Ann Arbor, MI: Servant Books, 1985.

Michael Kammen — *Spheres of Liberty: Changing Perspectives in American Culture*. Madison: The University of Wisconsin Press, 1986.

Martin Luther King Jr. — *Where Do We Go from Here—Chaos or Community?* Boston: Beacon Press, 1965.

Leonard W. Levy — *The Establishment Clause: Religion and the First Amendment*. New York: Macmillan, 1986.

Jules Lobel, ed. — *A Less Than Perfect Union: Radical Perspectives on the US Constitution*. New York: The Monthly Review Press, 1987.

Loren A. Lomasky — *Persons, Rights, and the Moral Community*. New York: Oxford University Press, 1987.

Richard P. McBrien — *Caesar's Coin: Religion and Politics in America*. New York: Macmillan, 1987.

Manning Marable — *Black American Politics: From the Washington Marches to Jesse Jackson*. London: Verso, 1985.

Martin E. Marty — *Religion and Republic*. Boston: Beacon Press, 1987.

National Coalition Against Censorship — *The Meese Commission Exposed*. New York: National Coalition Against Censorship, 1986.

Aryeh Neier — *Defending My Enemy: American Nazis, the Skokie Case, and the Risks of Freedom*. New York: E.P. Dutton, 1979.

Edwin S. Newman & Daniel S. Moretti — *Civil Liberty and Civil Rights*. New York: Oceana Publications, 1987.

Joseph Perkins, ed. — *A Conservative Agenda for Black Americans*. Washington, DC: The Heritage Foundation, 1987.

Leo Pfeffer — *Religion, State, and the Burger Court*. Buffalo, NY: Prometheus Books, 1984.

Alphonso Pinkney — *The Myth of Black Progress*. New York: Cambridge University Press, 1984.

A. James Reichley — *Religion in American Public Life*. Washington, DC: The Brookings Institution, 1985.

W. Cleon Skousen — *The Making of America*. Washington, DC: National Center for Constitutional Studies, 1985.

Thomas Sowell — *Civil Rights: Rhetoric or Reality?* New York: William Morrow and Company, Inc., 1984.

Thomas Sowell — *The Economics and Politics of Race*. New York: William Morrow and Company, Inc., 1983.

Juan Williams — *Eyes on the Prize*. New York: Viking Penguin Inc., 1987.

Walter E. Williams — *The State Against Blacks*. New York: McGraw-Hill, 1982.

William Julius Wilson — *The Declining Significance of Race*. Chicago: University of Chicago Press, 1975.

William Julius Wilson — *The Truly Disadvantaged: The Inner-City, the Underclass, and Public Policy*. Chicago: University of Chicago Press, 1987.

James E. Wood Jr., ed. — *Religion and the State: Essays in Honor of Leo Pfeffer*. Waco, TX: Baylor University Press, 1985.

Index

227